W9-DET-252

HOLDING *the* LINE

A LIFETIME OF DEFENDING
DEMOCRACY AND AMERICAN VALUES

RONNY JACKSON

Post Hill
PRESS

A POST HILL PRESS BOOK
ISBN: 978-1-63758-020-2
ISBN (eBook): 978-1-63758-021-9

Holding the Line:
A Lifetime of Defending Democracy and American Values
© 2022 by Ronny Jackson
All Rights Reserved

Cover photo by White House Photographer Myles Cullen
Cover design by Cody Corcoran

This is a work of nonfiction. All people, locations, events, and situations
are portrayed to the best of the author's memory.

Post Hill Press
New York • Nashville
posthillpress.com

Published in the United States of America
1 2 3 4 5 6 7 8 9 10

Dedicated to my wife, Jane.
My friend, my inspiration, my partner,
my soulmate, my protector, and my biggest fan.
The only person who really knows me and the one person
I can always count on no matter what happens.
I love you!

INTRODUCTION

January 6, 2021: Washington, DC

By the morning of January 6, I had already decided how I was going to vote on the House floor later that day. I had made up my mind. I wasn't one of those people on the fence. I was going to object to the certification of the Electoral College votes.

The Constitution says that the state legislatures for each state will determine the conduct of the election. That's it. The state legislatures. And in my judgment, that is not what happened in the 2020 election.

You had everyone from governors and secretaries of state down to county clerks, judges, and other election officials who had decided weeks before the November 3 election that they were going to change election laws in their states. In my mind, this was specifically done so that they could justify unsolicited mail-in ballots, knowing that they could harvest ballots from that point forward and manipulate the vote to win the election—which is exactly what happened.

When I went to sleep on election night, President Trump was winning handily. He was up big in states like Florida and Texas, as well as other traditionally blue states that President Trump had won four years earlier: Michigan, Wisconsin, and Pennsylvania. So when I went to bed that night, it was obvious to me that he was going to win the election.

Then, in the wee hours of the night, the ballots started coming in from everywhere. Truckloads of them were delivered in certain Democrat-controlled cities, and they were counted with little to no oversight. Suddenly, the vote started changing, and Biden started taking the lead in some of these places. From that point forward, I felt confident that there was some level of fraud involved that needed to immediately be investigated. As the weeks and months have passed, it is even more obvious to me that that was the case.

I was hoping the fraud would be uncovered and the final vote tallies would be corrected, but it pretty quickly became obvious that it wasn't going to happen that way. Once the liberal press called the election for Biden, there was no way they were going back. They were no longer interested in the truth, and they wanted the American people to simply drink their Kool-Aid and move on.

Even some Republicans who had always publicly supported the president started to waiver. These were the Republicans who liked the way things were before Trump arrived at the White House. They thrived in the swamp, and they liked the way the swamp operated because they understood it.

Then Mr. Trump came to Washington and turned everything upside down.

Old power players from both the Left and the Right came together after the 2020 election, and it was obvious that they were covering up and undermining any efforts to investigate what really happened.

On January 6, I knew there weren't going to be enough votes to overturn the election. The Democrats had a majority in both the House and the Senate, and there were plenty of Republicans who had already made their mind up to certify the vote. None of that mattered to me, however. I still had an obligation to let my constituents know that even if the vote was not overturned, their voices would be heard through me, their representative in the people's house. I would do the right thing and let the rest of America know that those in the Thirteenth Congressional District of Texas were NOT okay with this. This was not acceptable and will never happen again. In addition, I felt it was my constitutional duty to oppose if I thought the votes weren't legitimate and were unconstitutional, and I did.

Some people in my district thought the election would be overturned, but I had to be realistic. I was one of those people who, every time I had a conversation with my constituents, said, "Look, we can pray for a miracle. Maybe something that we don't know about will come out between now and the sixth, and it will change the math. But right now, the math in the House and the Senate says this election is not going to be overturned. That being said, it's still important to have our voices heard and to be engaged in the process."

Based on principle, it was vital to make sure the rest of the country knew that in Texas, we felt like we were disenfranchised by the fraud that we believe took place in the election. For me, this wasn't about overturning the election to give it back to President Trump, although I would have been very pleased with that outcome. But when it came time to vote, I thought it was the right thing to do because I believed the Constitution had been violated by the states in question, and it was my duty as a representative in Congress to say so.

To their credit, Republican leadership in the House did not tell anybody how to vote on this issue. They had gotten the Republican Conference together for a meeting the day before the vote, and it was very productive. Members got up, representing both sides of the issue, making arguments for why we should or shouldn't certify the vote. Both sides made passionate arguments, but I felt like there was only one legitimate constitutional way forward. I felt like the right answer was to contest the certification of the electoral vote from the states in question.

I thought leaders McCarthy and Scalise did a great job not strong-arming anybody to vote a certain way. They understood that this was one of the most significant votes that any of us would ever make. Both of them said that they'd been in Congress for many years, and this was the most consequential vote they'd ever personally been confronted with. This carried the significance of something like voting to declare war. Everyone needed to approach this with the utmost seriousness.

They said, "Vote with your conscience. Vote for your district. Everybody's going to do what they feel like they've got to do, but we're not going to attack each other, and we're going to respect each other's votes."

I walked out of that meeting thinking: *If another member of my party, even a colleague from Texas, decides to vote in a different manner than I do, I'm not going to criticize them. I'm going to try to respect the fact that they voted the way they did, and I am going to assume they voted their conscience and the way their constituents expected them to.*

That's what I was doing, and I would expect that from them regarding my vote.

* * *

On the morning of January 6, the president was supposed to speak at a rally on the Ellipse near the White House. I had several constituents that were close friends of mine who were planning to be there, so I thought I would go down there and say hi and see what was going on. I also figured I would see a lot of friends from the White House Military Office, Secret Service, and President Trump's staff who I had worked closely with over the past few years. He was scheduled to speak at eleven in the morning, but he was running late. A member of my staff and I went down there, but it took much longer to get there than I anticipated due to all the closed streets. We got there just before eleven o'clock. In the crowd that morning were thousands of people wearing Trump hats, carrying American flags and Trump flags, and all kinds of other patriotic and Trump paraphernalia. It was an incredibly peaceful and festive atmosphere. Everybody was in a great mood. People had their kids with them and were soaking up the atmosphere and the nice weather.

Unfortunately, I couldn't stay long. I figured as soon as the president started speaking, I would have to sneak away. But he was running late, and I couldn't find the constituents I was looking for anyway. I ended up leaving the Ellipse around 11:15 a.m. or so because I knew it would take us at least thirty minutes to get back to the floor of the House, where I needed to be by noon. I recorded a quick social media video telling people in my district, "Hey, we're out here...a lot of great Trump supporters are out here. We're supporting our president and our Constitution, and now I'm heading back to the floor for the vote today on the certification of the Electoral College results." That was it. I saw absolutely nothing that was the least bit concerning or worrisome.

We headed to Capitol Hill, and I took a seat in the back of the House Chamber. The Senate came in, and the joint session began. Both the House and the Senate started going through the states in alphabetical order. When we got to Arizona, both the House and the Senate made a motion to contest the legitimacy of the electoral vote for that state. So, at that point, the Senate broke away to go back to their chamber, and members of the House stayed on the floor of the House. Following the rules, the Senate and the House would debate among themselves in their own chambers for the next two hours and then get back together at the end. After this, both the Senate and House would take a final vote on whether we would certify Arizona. Unfortunately, I already knew that even after the debate period, we would not have the required votes to prevent Arizona's electoral votes from being certified. I was hoping for a miracle. But at this point, it seemed strictly procedural. As I have said before, I still believed it was necessary and important. I knew how I was voting!

In the House, we started debating. Somebody from the Republican side stood up and spoke, and then somebody from the Democrat side got up and answered. This went back and forth for about an hour. Initially, Nancy Pelosi was standing at the podium, presiding over it all.

Suddenly, out of nowhere, the Capitol police entered the chamber, and they did so in a very disruptive way. They came in making a lot of noise and started shutting all the doors. *Boom, boom, boom!* All the doors shut, and you could hear the locking of the doors. *Click, click, click, click!*

The police stayed in the chamber, weapons drawn. One of them went up on the podium, got Pelosi's attention, and Pelosi quickly left, and somebody else came in to replace her. The representative speaking at the time asked the Speaker to restore order to the floor of the House, not fully understanding what was happening.

Pat Fallon, one of my colleagues, was sitting next to me and said, "I wonder if there's a bomb threat?" There had already been a couple of bomb threats in the House office buildings earlier in the day, and my staff had already been evacuated from the Cannon office building and then readmitted, so it was a natural first thought.

But I knew it wasn't a bomb threat because the police wouldn't have locked us in the chamber on the floor of the house and posted themselves inside with weapons. I had spent fourteen years at the White House working with the Secret Service and other protective details, and it was clear to me that someone was inside the Capitol who shouldn't be there. Unfortunately, my first impression turned out to be right.

Right about that time, I heard a *boom, boom, boom, boom, BOOM!* It sounded like it was far away, but not really *that* far away. I knew what it was because I'd heard it many times during my military service. It was tear gas being deployed. You could also hear lots of yelling in the distance. You couldn't tell what was being said, but it sounded threatening.

At that time, the House leadership at the podium told everyone to "remain calm, but please get your gas masks out. There are people in the Capitol that are not supposed to be here. We may have to evacuate, and we may have to go through the area where tear gas has been deployed."

It was then that I knew they were losing control of what was going on. I mean, if they were deploying tear gas inside the Capitol, it was obvious they had lost control.

Everybody has escape hoods (they're not really gas masks) underneath their seats in the chamber, and most members didn't even know they were there. I'd seen the "masks" when I'd first gotten to the House Chamber days before and was just looking around. Thanks to all the time I had spent in the White House, I'd already had extensive training with these particular "masks." So I got mine out and opened it up quickly.

I didn't immediately pull my mask out of its box, as this would have started the electric blower inside. When they come on, they generate filtered, clean air for you to breathe. So, I left mine unwrapped but in the box and ready to go.

At that point, I noticed several members near me didn't know how to use the hoods. So, I went around and started showing other members how to open their masks and properly pull them over their heads. Then suddenly, we heard banging. *Bang, bang, bang!* They were beating on the back door of the House Chamber. This is the door opposite the speaker's area and the Speaker's Lobby. It is the door closest to the entrance of Statuary Hall. That's when I thought, *They are actually here, and they are on the other side of the door, and they are coming in!* That's when it got real. That's when I started to smell the tear gas from the other side of the door. There was lots of banging and yelling, and it was getting louder every second. At this point, we had no idea who was on the other side of the door. Based on what was going on, I didn't really care. All I knew was they were about to break the door down. We had been in the middle of the debate when all this started. And things were so crazy and happening so fast, I never even thought to use my phone to look online and get a perspective from the outside of the chamber.

By now, I was running on pure adrenaline, trying to problem-solve and focus on what to do next. Everyone on the floor started to run to the other side of the chamber near the Speaker's Lobby. Most started going into the Speaker's Lobby. I had been sitting in the back with my new colleagues from Texas right near the door that was about to be breached when this whole thing started. We all realized right away that the Capitol police officers there were about to be badly outnumbered when that door burst open. There were initially only about three officers there in front of the door with their weapons drawn. At that point, I, along with fellow Texas House members Pat Fallon, Troy Nehls, Tony Gonzales, and Markwayne Mullin from Oklahoma, a member I hadn't really met yet, decided we weren't going anywhere. None of us were going to leave these guys here to deal with this by themselves.

The door began shaking violently to the point where it started to buckle. It was obvious that the mob was ramming something into the door, or they were throwing the weight of their bodies into it. It looked like it was about to burst open any second.

That was when Pat, Troy, Tony, Markwayne, and I looked for objects to block the door. We started grabbing furniture. We got some big heavy pieces four or five feet long and dragged them in front of the door.

The two or three Capitol police officers had handguns, but that was it. We didn't have anything. We decided we better be able to help these Capitol police officers when that mob comes through the door.

There was nothing readily available to use as a weapon, so we started breaking the legs off furniture. There were a couple of hand sanitizer stations that had long wooden posts on them, so we broke those off their bases to make clubs.

Pat Fallon looked over at me and Tony Gonzales and said, "Hey, take your tie off so they can't choke you with it."

I had forgotten I was wearing a tie, but I quickly said, "That's a good thought. I'm taking that dang thing off.… I don't want to get choked with my own tie." I took it off, threw it aside, and we lined up behind the police officers with our wooden clubs.

I've had people ask me, "Well, why didn't you guys just run and get out of there?" Well, it really was that primal fight-or-flight sensation that kicked in. I've been in situations like this before, having served twenty-five years on active duty in the United States Navy. I've been in harm's way and know firsthand what it feels like to be in a combat zone. Needless to say, I did not think this is what it would be like to serve in Congress. Nevertheless, here we were in this unique and unprecedented situation. If you looked around, there was nowhere to go. I mean, we were locked inside the House Chamber and appeared to be surrounded, so flight was not an option. At that point, it was pretty obvious "fight" was the only option left. So we were fighting!

The reality is we didn't really have anywhere to go at that point. The Capitol police had made the determination that it was safer to keep the roughly two hundred members locked inside the chamber rather than try to evacuate us through unsecured routes and risk running into the mob. Good decision at the time!

Our thoughts were, *Hey, it looks like they're coming in any minute. When that door bursts open, we're going to fight like hell and do everything we can to convince them to turn around and not come any farther, and if that doesn't work, we are going to fight our way out of here. We will defend ourselves!*

(As a side note, I don't recall any Democrats standing with us. Not even one. Republican members of Congress were the only ones who were ready to fight.)

Once we got the furniture lined up, I found myself standing beside the glass window of the chamber door with a makeshift wooden stick in my hand for protection. I bent down to knock a piece of wood off the end of the club I had made, and as I looked up, I heard a pop, and projectiles immediately came through the glass.

Now, to this day, I'm almost certain somebody fired shots through that window. (Markwayne Mullin was there with me, and he didn't think there were shots fired; he thought they were using a glass punch to bust the glass.) The Capitol police have also indicated that no shots were fired to their knowledge. What I saw was a blast of glass dust coming from the window and the simultaneous popping sound of what I thought was gunfire. Regardless, I was not the only one who thought that. Two or three of the officers simultaneously yelled, "SHOTS FIRED!" And everybody got down.

That was when the Capitol police decided that it was safer to get us out of there and move us through a potentially unsecured evacuation route versus keeping us in the chamber. They opened the outer door to the Speaker's Lobby, and everyone started moving out. At that point, I started moving to the other side of the chamber and into the Speaker's Lobby.

In the Speaker's Lobby, there are two doors: one on the right and one on the left, separated by thirty or forty feet. The rioters were about to break through the door on the left, where we later learned a young lady, Ashli Babbitt, was shot. We took the door to the right and quickly moved down a flight of stairs to a safe location. We got out of there just in the nick of time.

As soon as we got to a secure location, I picked my phone up and called every member of my family. My mom and dad were at home in Texas. My wife was at our home in Silver Spring. My daughter was at work in the DC area. My oldest son was in California on active duty. And my youngest son was attending school in Maryland.

I knew they were watching the TV and were terrified by what they were seeing. They asked, "Where are you? Are you okay?" I told them that I was fine and in a safe location but couldn't tell them much more than that, as it would be ridiculous to discuss specific locations. The main reason we were in a secure and safe location was because it was undisclosed. (Unfortunately, some members of Congress and staff members were speaking to reporters and telling them exactly where we were.)

* * *

On January 6, violent people on both the Far Right and the Far Left traveled to the Capitol to cause as much chaos and trouble as possible. Anyone who planned and instigated this needs to be identified and held accountable for their actions.

The people who attacked Capitol police officers need to be held accountable. You simply just don't do that to the great men and women of our law enforcement. Likewise, the people who destroyed property also need to be held accountable. The people who broke into the offices of Nancy Pelosi and Kevin McCarthy need to be held accountable.

However, the government's response should be justified and reasonable. You can't take these people and destroy their lives, families, and livelihoods simply because they are deemed "Trump supporters." This is exactly what the Left is trying to do. We can't do that. It must be a measured response based on the actions of each individual, and anyone accused of a crime must be afforded due process and fair treatment through the normal judicial system. This is not what is happening with many of those who have been accused and arrested. This is a fundamental right as an American citizen, and our government under the Biden administration has denied this in many cases. This is shameful, illegal, and un-American—and this cannot stand!

There were also thousands of patriotic Americans who were exercising their First Amendment right to speak out, support President Trump, and question the results of the election. These people did nothing wrong, and they should not be blamed or grouped in with anyone who broke the law that day at the Capitol.

Let me also be clear: I don't blame President Trump at all for the events on January 6.

President Trump specifically said during his speech that day, "I know that everyone here will soon be marching over to the Capitol building to peacefully and patriotically make your voices heard." He repeatedly referenced the crowd's plan to walk down Pennsylvania Avenue and let members of Congress hear their voices and show their support for Republicans who were about to cast votes on the validity of the electoral college results. He never once suggested they do anything else. The Left likes to reference the fact that Trump used the word "fight" in his speech. Specifically, when he said, "We fight like hell. And if you don't fight like hell, you're not going to have a country anymore." He said this while talking about future election security and his administration's ongoing efforts to find out what really happened in some of the states in question. It had nothing to do with the events of the day. The fact that they are fixated on the word "fight" is ridiculous. Every politician, including myself, uses the word "fight." Fight for your Second Amendment, fight for your First Amendment, fight for pro-life legislation. The Left uses it just as much as the Right does. They took that one word and said, "He incited a riot!" The president did no such thing.

Try as they might, the Left cannot hang this around President Trump's neck in any shape, form, or fashion. The protestors who forced their way into the Capitol crossed the line in a big way. You don't go to the Capitol and threaten the lives of members of Congress.

If you want to protest, you protest peacefully. I'm disgusted with the actions that transpired that day, and I am disgusted with the Left's constant attempt to use it for political gain.

I'm also secure in my belief that President Trump didn't have a damn thing to do with it!

1.

*"I've traveled all over the world, but I don't think
there is any place better than Texas."*
—Red Adair

B elieve it or not, I can trace the Jackson family all the way back to the year 992. Sounds crazy, but it's not. Most of that time, my family lived in England, where they kept meticulous birth, marriage, and death records, so it wasn't as hard as I thought it would be.

I discovered they were originally Norman from the Normandy region of France, and they came over with William the Conqueror in the Battle of Hastings in 1066. They settled there and stayed in England until about 1630.

Eventually, they made their Atlantic crossing and ended up in the soon-to-be United States of America. They migrated from the northeast part of the country, where they landed, and eventually ended up in Mississippi. That is where my grandfather was born and raised. He moved to Texas when he was a young man with the hopes of becoming a cowboy, but he ended up being a carpenter and a schoolteacher instead. He was the first Jackson to call Texas home.

I arrived on the scene on May 4, 1967. I was born in Lubbock, Texas, but lived in Levelland, a tiny little town in Hockley County, mostly comprised of rural cotton farmers and folks who work in the oil and gas industry. Levelland was, and still is, your typical small, tight-knit West Texas community, filled with God-fearing, hardworking, patriotic Americans who always take care of each other.

I come from a long line of tough, gritty blue-collar workers. My father, Waymon, is an electrician, and my mother, Norma, is a homemaker. My dad can literally do anything: he can do electrical work, he is a master plumber, he is a pretty good mechanic, and he can build or fix practically anything you can think of. He owned an electrical business with his twin brother Raymon. The two of them were affectionately referred to by everyone in town as "the Jackson brothers" or "the Jackson twins."

My dad would leave for work at eight in the morning and not come home until one or two the following morning. He and my mother worked hard to give me, my little brother Gary, and my little sister Stacy everything we needed. I definitely grew up in an environment with a strong emphasis on work ethic, where you were expected to work for anything you needed. If I wanted more than the essentials, I had to earn it with the sweat of my labor. I spent a lot of time working with my dad on the weekends and after school. By the time I was fourteen, I had a full-time job of my own. When I say full-time, I mean thirty to sixty hours a week, every single week. Both my parents are responsible for instilling this solid work ethic in me, which is a big part of why I'm where I am today.

My career started at the movie theater, running the concession area, where I would do everything, including count the money and take it to the bank. At thirteen years old, I was managing a large part of the operation. By the time I was fourteen, I was working at the United Supermarket, stocking, sacking, checking, and doing anything that needed to be done. I never complained and never said no to any job.

Since work and football practice started at the same time after school, I had to decide early on what my priorities were. I couldn't do both. It was a rather easy decision on my end since I never was that great at sports. When I was really young, I played baseball, football, soccer, basketball—all that kind of stuff. I could run fast and had a lot of cardiovascular endurance, but I didn't have great coordination or any natural athletic ability. Thankfully, I didn't come from a family of athletes, and there was never any pressure for me to become an athlete. The pressure in my family was to get a job and work hard. That really was what my family was all about: working hard.

So I decided it was more important for me to have a car, clothes, and other necessary things I wanted than to play football, and as a result, I went to work full-time after school. I would clock in to work at four in the afternoon and clock out at ten thirty or eleven every night, then get up to go to school the next day. I'd do that every day, Monday through Friday. Then on the weekends, I would work ten-to-twelve-hour shifts on Saturday and after church on Sunday.

At fourteen years old, I even got my hardship driver's license. I spoke with a judge and got a note stating that I needed it to get to work. I paid for my car too. My dad took me to an auto auction in Lubbock, and I bought a Pontiac Grand LeMans. I think I paid four thousand dollars for it, but I didn't have all the money. So I put a thousand dollars down, and then my dad took me to the bank and got a loan for the rest in my name. I was fifteen years old and already had car and insurance payments.

While in school, I was always a bit of a class clown. I got in a lot of trouble when I was growing up. For most of my youth, I was considered the black sheep in my deeply conservative family. My folks and most of my relatives didn't drink, smoke, dance.… I mean, it was very, very conservative, and that's the environment I was raised in. I was always getting into my fair share of trouble, and my dad was always out looking for me, trying to figure out where I was, what I was doing, and why I didn't come home when I was supposed to. It didn't help that I worked and had my own money. I know I caused a lot of problems for my mom and dad growing up, but I'm glad I was able to make amends for that and eventually turn things around.

My dad didn't want me to fight and encouraged me not to do so. However, he didn't want me getting picked on either. And he wanted me to defend myself when I needed to. He thought I should learn that there are better ways to solve things. Unfortunately, I did get in quite a few fights growing up. Fighting in school back then was much less dangerous than today in most public schools. The worst that could happen is you get beat up a little and sent to the principal's office. The principal would make you shake hands and then give you a choice between taking three licks with the paddle or calling your parents and potentially being suspended for a couple of days.

I got beat to death with that paddle because I never wanted my parents to find out about anything. I knew the punishment I would get at home would be much worse. I had a principal, Mr. Goodnight, and a couple of coaches who were so big and strong, I remember my feet coming off the ground when I got paddled. I would go home at night, and the next day, my butt cheeks would be black and blue, but it was still better than explaining it to my dad.

Although I got into quite a few scuffles in school, I had lots of terrific friends throughout grade school, junior high, and high school. Typical of most small towns, everyone knew everyone's business.

College wasn't a given for me. I only started thinking about going to college because all my friends were going. Most of my friends either went to Texas Tech or away to another school, and I couldn't afford either. So, I decided to enroll at South Plains College, the junior college in my hometown. I also started working in the oil field at that time in order to pay for it all. My dad didn't want to discourage me from going to school, but he still thought it was ultimately a waste of money and time. He asked me at one point when I was going to give up on college. He said, "Get out in the oil field full time; start making some money. You could be gaining seniority right now. You could be a foreman in a few years."

I could totally see my dad's point, but I was driven by curiosity and the sense that I needed to explore my options and do something else. I knew the little town that I grew up in, and that was about it. I had no direction and no idea what I wanted to do. Turns out, that was the best decision of my early life.

I started as an engineering major and quickly discovered that wasn't my thing.

I was great at math and had been a good student in high school, though I had skipped school a lot. I continually called in sick to school, and my mom would cover for me. Sometimes, she would call in for me and say, "Ronny is not feeling well." Which was true: I did not feel well. I was not getting much sleep. After all, I was working a full-time job, and I was exhausted. I had a hard time getting up sometimes, and my mom just felt terrible for me.

Despite missing school, a lot, I made excellent grades. You wouldn't be able to get away with skipping that much school nowadays because you wouldn't graduate. When I walked across my high school stage at graduation, my principal, Mr. Baggett, looked frustrated when he handed me my diploma because I had missed so much school. He congratulated everybody, but when he gave me mine, he said, "Okay, Jackson, you can stay home and sleep every day now."

Because I wasn't planning to go to college, I scrambled to get in. I never took the SAT or the ACT. I called the junior college, and they said they'd let me enroll if I took the ACT the following semester. I, of course, agreed, but I never took it, and it never came up again. When I started college, I worked both in the oil field and at the supermarket, stocking groceries. I preferred the oil field because the money was a lot better, and I could work fewer hours. The tuition at my junior college at the time was thirteen dollars a semester hour. It was ridiculously cheap and affordable for me.

During high school, I didn't do anything but go to school and work. If I had any free time, I was spending it with a girlfriend. Despite going to school, I only had two interests in high school: work and girls. That was it. Once I started college, I eventually added school to my list of priorities.

I was working to pay for the things I wanted, but I was also pitching in when the family needed it. My mom borrowed money from me frequently. She had a pad of paper she used to keep a running total of what she owed me—a balance of two or three hundred dollars at a time. She always paid me back. She'd mark it off and pay me fifty back, and then she'd ask to borrow another fifty or so. My mom borrowed money from my brother and me all the time because we both had jobs. My dad was running a successful business, but when you own the business, you have to pay the bills before you pay yourself. He had to buy tractors, trucks, trailers, and all kinds of other equipment, as well as pay the mortgage on the company and the house. My parents were working their butts off to pay the bills. When I was younger, I never really realized why my mom went to the store every day. I learned later in life that it was because she had only enough money to buy food for dinner that night and maybe meals for the next day, and that was it.

Some weeks, my dad did well, and there was more money around; some weeks, there wasn't. That's part of owning your own business. My parents appreciated that I worked hard. My dad graduated from high school, but when he was young, anything beyond that was considered a waste of time and money. Academics was not a focus in my family in any shape, form, or fashion. The expectation was to get your high school degree, and then you'd go out, get a job, and make a good living for your family. That's what it was all about.

Most of my friends were excellent athletes. My best friend, Ronald, who lived down the street, was a high school quarterback and a fantastic basketball player. My dad built me a basketball hoop when I was little, so we were always in my front yard, shooting baskets or playing football. The big difference was he was good at it, and I wasn't. We didn't watch much television when I was growing up; to be honest, we only had three channels. No, we had four: ABC, CBS, NBC, and PBS. That was it. There was nothing for kids to watch on TV except for the Saturday morning cartoons, which we got up early to watch. Other than that, I didn't care about watching TV. I stayed outside almost all the time.

I've been on the news a fair amount over the past few years, so when I visit Levelland, most people know who I am and what I've done. They're still shocked that I was a rear admiral in the US Navy and was the White House physician for three presidents. That's mainly because I got into so much trouble when I was growing up.

What changed everything for me was my decision to go to junior college. Initially, I didn't like it too much because I had picked the wrong major. I was an engineering major but very quickly realized that it wasn't for me. I was very good at math and science, but the engineering graphics classes killed me. You must have the ability to see everything three-dimensionally, and for whatever reason I could not do that. I would sit in these graphics classes, and my classmates would come in, draw a three-dimensional nut and a bolt, and be done in thirty minutes. I'd sit there for two hours, trying to do it. I just could not see things three-dimensionally and translate them onto paper. I got frustrated and decided it wasn't for me. Fortunately, I soon found my calling: marine biology.

When I was in my mid-teens, I worked at United Supermarket. My best friend also worked there. He and I found out about a scuba diving course being taught in the evenings at the junior college in Levelland. We were both interested and signed up. Scuba diving around Levelland is challenging to say the least. As the name implies, it's flat as a board, but in addition, there's absolutely no water. It's an unlikely place to get into diving, but we decided we were going to do it. So, we enrolled in the class and became certified scuba divers.

We enjoyed it and quickly moved from the introductory class to the advanced and rescue diver classes. We were diving little spring-fed lakes and quarries all over Texas and New Mexico. When I finished high school and completed my first semester of college, I realized I still didn't know what I wanted to do for a career. I decided to sit out of college for a semester and work full time at the grocery store and some in the oil field. I worked sixty plus hours a week and tried to rack up as much overtime as possible.

My best friend and I saved our money that semester, and we booked a trip to Australia as backpackers. Once we got there, we signed up for a divemaster course and ultimately got jobs. We were over there on travel visas, so we weren't really allowed to be working. We spent two weeks out on the boat doing the divemaster course and did so well the guys that ran the dive shop said, "Do you guys want to work?" We said "Sure," and they put us right to work as divemasters on the boat.

My only job was to take the divers down, show them around during the day, do their dive tables to ensure they didn't get decompression sickness, fill their tanks, and make sure they stayed safe. I would then hang out with them at night and make sure they were entertained and having a good time. I worked for a company called South Pacific Divers, and as part of the deal, they let me live on the boat. We would leave early Monday morning and go way out on to the Great Barrier Reef and into the Coral Sea. The skipper would anchor on the reef somewhere, and we would dive all day. Every night, they would move the boat to a new location on the reef so we could dive somewhere new. We would stay out at sea until Friday evening and then come back to port. They would tie the boat up, and I would sleep there for the weekend. They gave me a little spending money so that I could go out in town and do a few things. The following Monday, I'd be back out at sea again, diving.

I worked as a divemaster in Australia for a few weeks that summer and then came back home. When I came back home, things had significantly changed for me because I knew exactly what I wanted to be and what I wanted to study in college. I had been an engineering major but changed my major to biology. My plan was to finish my biology degree at the junior college I was attending and then immediately transfer to Texas A&M University at Galveston and study marine biology. I made decent grades in high school, and I did okay the first semester of college, but I wasn't focused. Now that I was motivated and focused on what I wanted, I started killing it in school. I pretty much got a 4.0 every semester from that point forward. I finally had a plan!

Now that I am older and wiser, I am often asked to speak with groups of young people and tell them about my path and my career.

I always point out, you will go through many trials and tribulations in life, and you will get on the wrong path from time to time. You're either going to continue down the wrong path and self-destruct, or you're going to make the necessary course corrections to get you back on the right track. That is life! The only reason that I have spent more time on the right path than the wrong path, and the primary reason I have been successful in life, is because of my mom and dad.

How did your mom and dad do that, some might ask? First off, they are very principled and have a strong set of morals. They raised me in the Church of Christ, and I was taught early on the difference between right and wrong. They instilled it from birth, so I have always had a sharp conscience. When I was doing something wrong, I knew I was doing something wrong and that it wasn't okay. They not only taught me that, but they also gave me an incredible work ethic, a sense of personal responsibility, and respect for others. Unfortunately, I spent a lot of time on the wrong path early on in life and, as a result, made life miserable for my parents in the process. I feel bad about it today and wish I hadn't punished them like that early on. They wasted lots of time worrying about me. Eventually, the way my mom and dad raised me is what brought me back. I wouldn't have been able to turn it around if I didn't have that foundation, the foundation they laid, the one that kept me from going too far down the wrong path.

I'm the first person in my family to go to college, much less graduate from college. I realize how important it was that I had a mom and a dad who were with me all the way. My mother and father invested in my success and didn't give up on me.

I had definitely received a lot of attention for the bad things I had done growing up, but it turns out, I thrived on getting attention for the good things as well. Luckily, at this point in my life, I had already got many bad things out of my system. I was now motivated, focused, dedicated, and hardworking. I was still working full time, making a fair amount of money, and paying for my school and all of my expenses. As I stated earlier, I attended South Plains College, a tiny junior college in Levelland, where I grew up. I got an excellent education there, even better than at A&M because the classes were small and personal.

There was a lot of one-on-one time with the actual instructors, and you were not dealing with as many teaching assistants. You were dealing with the actual professors. I loved science, physics, chemistry, and math. I excelled academically and ended up going to Texas A&M at Galveston after I graduated from South Plains College, where I could pursue a marine biology degree. I initially joined the school's military corps, which is somewhat similar to the Corps of Cadets at Texas A&M main campus and part of the Texas Maritime Academy. I thought at the time this was a great fit since I had always been attracted to a career in the military as well. As a matter of fact, when I was nineteen years old and just before my trip to Australia, I had met with a recruiter in Coronado, California, and tried to enlist in the navy and go to BUD/S to become a Navy SEAL. Unfortunately, my vision was not within standards and that was off the table for me. Although I was disappointed, I was convinced that somehow, I would still find my way into the military in the near future.

Once in the corps, I wore a uniform to school every day, lined up every morning in formation for roll call, marched, did military drills, and worked on the ship. We had a huge 473-foot-long training ship called the *Texas Clipper*, which was an old World War II attack transport ship that the school owned and operated in order to train us as sailors. Everyone in this program at Texas A&M was a marine major of some sort: marine science, marine engineering, marine biology, or marine transportation. If you stayed in the Corps of Cadets and graduated from the Texas Maritime Academy, you had the option of going directly into the military or directly into the merchant marine fleet. If you chose the military route, it was similar to graduating from the Naval Academy, where you go straight into the navy as a surface warfare officer or an engineering officer.

You could also select the civilian sector option with the merchant marine fleet and ultimately work as a chief engineer or ship's captain. These are the people who drive the large commercial tankers and cargo ships.

After my first year there, I wasn't sure I wanted to do either. I decided I wanted to focus full time on marine biology, so I got out of the corps after my first year.

I was receiving some scholarship money that first year and was doing really well in the corps. Since I transferred with my associate's degree in biology, all my classes that first year at A&M were focused on catching up on the required maritime classes you have to take as a member of the corps and the Texas Maritime Academy. I took classes such as terrestrial navigation, seamanship, celestial navigation, oceanography, and maritime rules of the road. I could have stayed in the Corps of Cadets, and ultimately, I would have probably been the corps commander. But I came to A&M to study marine biology and decided I wanted to focus all my time on my marine biology curriculum. So that is exactly what I did; I finished and got my degree in marine biology.

Paying for college was a constant source of stress for me. I would go home on spring and Christmas breaks, and anytime I had more than three or four days off, and work in the oil field as much as possible to make a little extra money to pay for books, tuition, and fees for the next semester. I always had on-campus jobs as well. I worked in a chemistry lab running the gas chromatographer and in the marine biology lab feeding the stingrays, sharks, and turtles. However, my main job was working as a resident advisor at the university. This helped more than anything since part of my salary was free room and board. That left me with the responsibility for my tuition and everything else. Everything was going well, and I was making ends meet, but I didn't have much money to go out and entertain. This became a problem for me when I started dating my soon-to-be wife, Jane.

I'm three and a half years older than Jane. She was from Silver Spring, Maryland, and her father was a retired army surgeon. He had been an army cardiothoracic surgeon for twenty-eight years. He had done two tours in Vietnam in a MASH unit as a combat surgeon. After he retired from the military, he changed his medical profession and became a pathologist. Her mom and her dad divorced when she was about ten years old. Her father got remarried a couple of times but ultimately ended up living in Galveston, where he was working at the University of Texas Medical Branch in the pathology department.

After Jane graduated from high school, her father talked her into relocating to Texas and attending Texas A&M University at Galveston in order to spend some time with him during her freshman year. She didn't know what she wanted to ultimately study, but the move made sense since she qualified for in-state tuition and would be taking just basic courses during her first year anyway. He said, "Get your math, English, history, and all your basics completed and live here in Texas for a year or two. You'll have time to decide what you're going to do, and you can go off to college somewhere else if this is not where you want to be." So she enrolled at Texas A&M at Galveston, and I was the RA who checked her in to a room—that's how we met. She showed up, and I'd already been there for a couple of weeks, checking in students. There was a big party in her suitemates' room the night she got there.

Tons of people were there, including many of my friends from the corps. I walked her to her room to check her in. There were a bunch of people who had spilled into her room from the party next door. Somebody was sleeping, passed out in her bed. Her roommate was there and had been drinking a little too much, and Jane said, "This is crazy! I just got here, and there's already someone passed out in my bed!" Her roommate was also a little irritated at that point and wanted everybody out of their room. So long story short, I found another room for the two of them to sleep in that night; I got the party shut down, got everyone out of their rooms, and had everything cleaned up. We started dating soon after that, and although we broke up a few times, we eventually got married.

I was super popular; I knew everybody on campus. I was the RA, and I probably shouldn't say this, but I oversaw all the other RAs, and we kind of ran the place like the mafia. We weren't supposed to have any alcohol on campus or have parties. If you came in and talked to us first, and we blessed you, we might look the other way and let certain things happen. If you didn't, we might come to your room, confiscate your beer and liquor, and shut the party down. In other words, if you kissed the ring beforehand, we might let your party go on. I got along with everybody; we had lots of fun. I was very outgoing and spent a lot of time out, going to parties, going to the beach, and just hanging out with everyone. I had an outgoing personality, and I had tons of friends there. For better or worse, everybody on campus knew who I was.

It wasn't hard for me to make friends. It has always come naturally. I am very outgoing, and I like talking to people and being around other people. I have always been a pretty good storyteller and a little bit of an entertainer as well. I am very bored when I am by myself. Socializing is part of any university campus but especially on a small campus like Texas A&M at Galveston. We didn't have sports, so I spent a lot of my free time helping others with their studies. I enjoyed studying, and I was well respected on campus from an academic standpoint because I probably had one of the highest GPAs in the entire school.

I should say that I do not consider myself to be exceptionally smart. I am of average intelligence, but I do have an exceptional work ethic. I got good grades the hard way: I worked for them. Part of my academic success was derived from the fact that it made my parents proud for a change, and that was important to me.

Making my parents proud and proving I could excel in school was definitely what motivated me the most early on. However, as time went on, I realized I was doing it for myself; by the time I got to Texas A&M, I was doing it because I knew I could, and I knew it was key to my future. I couldn't accept that I might be getting a B in a class when I knew damn well that if I just devoted a little bit more time studying the subject matter, I could easily get an A, and that's what I did. Plain and simple, I worked my butt off and made excellent grades. It's the way I've always been; once I get into something, it's 110 percent. All or nothing!

I don't have many regrets in my career, but one thing I do regret is not taking the time to enjoy the ride a little more. I am not very good at enjoying the moment. I'm instantly thinking about the next step as soon I accomplish something. I find myself quickly making calculations and thinking, *Where does that leave me, what am I doing next, and how do I get there?* It definitely makes you more successful, but it also plagues you a little because you don't enjoy what you're doing to the fullest. The older I've become, the more I've learned to step back and make myself take account of what's going on around me and enjoy what's happening. But when I was younger, as soon as I hit one rung on the ladder, I was looking for the next rung, and it was relentless.

I'm not to the point where I am sitting around, feeling self-actualized, completely content, and like I've achieved everything in life that's out there for me. I'm not there yet; maybe I will be someday, someday soon—hopefully, maybe in the next ten years or so. I always feel like there's something else I could or should do, something else meaningful, fun, or satisfying. There's having success, and there's feeling successful. They are two separate things, and they don't always go together.

I think some of the most successful people in life don't always feel that sense of success. They always feel like they're falling just a little bit short, and they can be just a little bit better, and to be honest with you, I'm that way. I drive my staff crazy right now because I'm always talking about how I could have done better every time I do something. Even when the overwhelming consensus is that I did an excellent job, it doesn't always feel like it. They tell me that I'm unbelievably hard on myself, but that's just how I am, and I can't help it. Probably not the healthiest trait I have, but one that is hard to overcome.

My dad was a sergeant in the Army National Guard when he was very young. But other than that, I didn't have any immediate family members in the military. I did have an uncle who was in the army in World War II. He was my dad's older brother, but I didn't know him well. I grew up relatively close to Reese Air Force Base, so I had a little exposure to that branch of the military. The one thing I didn't have, was any insight or influence from anyone regarding the US Navy. Most things in Texas that are related to the military revolve around the air force, especially where I lived. Maybe there's a little bit of the army in other parts of Texas, but the navy? Mostly no. Had it not been for my unlikely affection for scuba diving at an early age and my time working on a dive boat in Australia, I probably would have never considered joining the navy.

After my first year at A&M, I started dating my wife, and I needed to make a little bit of extra money. I was working as a resident advisor and in a couple of the biology labs. I was making ends meet, but when I met Jane, I developed a need to go out more and spend a little money on her. I didn't have that kind of money, so I started looking for other work.

I think we both knew we were going to end up together right off the bat. I was more aggressive about it up front, and Jane had a boyfriend back in Maryland. She was dealing with the fact that she had a boyfriend and I'd asked her out, so the first few times we went out, she kept her distance. She started to become interested in me, and then eventually, it was apparent that this boyfriend had to go, that she was going to be with me. At this point, I really needed a little extra money, so I went across the bridge to the University of Texas Medical Branch (UTMB), the medical school there in Galveston.

UTMB was the first and is the main medical school of the University of Texas. The University of Texas has four medical schools; they also have ones in Houston, Dallas, and San Antonio. Galveston is the biggest and the traditional medical school of the University of Texas.

I spoke to some professors there and said, "Do you have anything I could do over here when I'm not in class in order to make a little extra money?" I said I'd love to work in one of the chemistry or biology labs. They said they had a work-study program, and the administrators had just been complaining that the med students weren't taking advantage of this program; since I was a student at a state school, they said maybe we could work something out and they could get me a job working in one of the labs. I said, "Okay, that sounds great."

So, they called me back a few days later and said, "We got you a job, but you're going to be working in the pathology department." I said, "Okay," and then they told me I was going to be an autopsy assistant. I was like, "An autopsy assistant? That's not what I was planning to do, but I'll do it." So even though working as an autopsy assistant was not something I anticipated, and I had no idea what the job entailed, I agreed and took the job. To my surprise, my job was to do a big part of the autopsy. I would cut the patient open, assist in taking the organs out: the liver, the heart, the lungs. When we were done, I would close the body up and clean everything.

It wasn't traumatic for me. In Levelland, growing up, I was on the volunteer fire department by the time I was seventeen years old. The entire Jackson family was part of the volunteer fire department. Levelland had six paid firefighters and twenty-five volunteers; almost half the volunteers were Jacksons. I did that for three or four years. I went to a lot of car wrecks and fires and witnessed a fair amount of death in the process.

The pathology department did take some getting used to, however—predominantly due to the unusual smells involved. They were not normal smells and were mostly unpleasant. I was a little grossed out by the aromas, but I wasn't grossed out by handling the organs and the body itself. I would open the body up, remove the organs, cut and peel the scalp back, and then I would use a bone saw to cut the top of the skull off and take the brain out. I would then pass everything down to the pathology residents at the end of the table, and they would dissect everything and determine the cause of death. It's a bit creepy at first, but it didn't make me nauseated or sick, and you get used to it quickly.

When I first started, I had no interest in medicine, so being a doctor never crossed my mind, not one single time ever in my entire life. I hadn't been thinking about going to med school. But the pathology residents started teaching me. They would say, "Do you remember that liver you took out yesterday? Come down here and look at this one. This guy's got liver cancer. See the difference?" They started teaching me anatomy saying, "This is the gallbladder, and this is the pancreas." They started teaching me all kinds of things, and I thought it was very interesting. That's the very first time that I ever thought I might want to be a doctor. It came out of nowhere because of that experience.

I went in there just thinking it was another job. I initially would have rather spent that time working in a chemistry lab, running a gas chromatographer, or doing something else that was more up my lane. But I was being intellectually stimulated and thought it was fascinating. Every day, you go in there and gown up; you put a mask on, put a hat on, you put your face shield on. Bone saws are buzzing, and blood and guts are literally all over the place. It's crazy, but once I got in there, saw what was going on, and began learning, I knew I wanted to be a doctor.

I started getting more serious about it each and every day. As I began to explore a life in medicine, I quickly realized that I didn't want to be a pathologist because it didn't fit my personality. Every medical specialty has a personality that dominates it, and pathology is not my personality at all. I wanted to be either a trauma surgeon or an emergency medicine doctor, and I chose to be a trauma surgeon. However, I ended up being an emergency medicine doctor because I got married and had a family. As I was going through medical school, I realized that I didn't know a single trauma surgeon who wasn't divorced multiple times and who knew their kids. I didn't think I could be a family person and a trauma surgeon at the same time, so I ended up being an emergency medicine doctor, which turned out to be an outstanding fit and a great decision. Emergency medicine appealed to me since I had been a firefighter for a while, and I'd worked with EMTs and paramedics and seen these physicians in action in the hospital.

I decided to go to med school at the very last minute. I signed up for the MCAT about a week before the deadline. I didn't study for the MCAT one single day. I just walked in and took it cold. I thought it was a disaster. It was brutal. I went in there at seven thirty in the morning; we started testing, and we went all the way until six o'clock in the evening. We didn't have any breaks; we had maybe thirty minutes for lunch.

In every single section of the test, they would say, "You have one minute," and I'd think, *I still have thirty questions I haven't answered yet!* I would answer "BBBB," and then I'd get to the next section, and I'd be running one minute short again, and I would answer "BBBB" again. I walked out of that thing thinking I did horrible. I thought there was no way in hell I was going to med school now. I was bummed out and sure my plan to become a doctor was doomed!

Well, it turns out, I didn't do as bad as I thought I did. I ended up in the sixtieth percentile, which isn't great, but it's above average. But what saved me was that back then—I don't know how they do it now; I think they do it differently now—they weighed your MCAT and your GPA from college about fifty-fifty. My MCAT wasn't great, but it wasn't bad. But my GPA was like 3.93 from Texas A&M University; that's an excellent GPA. So long story short, I got in.

I only applied to in-state schools because I knew I could never afford to go out of state. I was already thinking, *How am I going to pay for this?* There was just no way I could pay for med school. I had gone out and worked in the oil field and raised enough money to go to Texas A&M, but medical school is a different ball game altogether.

I was stressing about how I was going to come up with the money. My parents didn't have money to help me, and I could not and would not borrow that kind of money. I knew people who had grad-uated medical school and owed somewhere between $150,000 and $200,000. I was like, *There's no way in hell I'm going to med school and getting out over $200,000 in debt; that's insane.* My dad had instilled in me early on in life that if you don't have the money to pay for it, you probably don't need it. My family didn't borrow money; it's just something we didn't do unless there were no other options. So, I was trying to figure out how to do this, and I thought to myself, *Well, you know what?* I had been in the corps at A&M. Maybe the military had a medical school, and they would look at other things besides my MCAT scores, because I was still worried about my MCAT scores, and if so, that might address my financial concerns as well.

I reached out to the recruiters in Houston for the army, the navy, and the air force and asked if they had a military medical school. They told me they didn't have a military medical school, which is a lie; they do. It's the Uniformed Services University of the Health Sciences in Bethesda. Either they didn't know that, or they didn't want me to know that because it wasn't the product they were selling. So instead, they said, "Look, here's the deal. If you get into medical school, we may be able to pay for it. You can get into any medical school in the fifty states, and we have a scholarship; you can apply for our scholarship, and we'll pay for your medical school, but you got to get in first."

I applied only to Texas schools because I thought that if I didn't get the military scholarship, there was no way I could afford to go out of state; that was inconceivable. I got accepted at every school I applied to except for one.

I got into three of the University of Texas schools, Texas A&M, and Texas Tech. I had to decide where I wanted to go. My parents wanted me to go to Texas Tech in Lubbock, about thirty miles east of where I grew up, so that I could live close to home. I thought about it, and it had an excellent reputation, but it didn't have the prestige of the University of Texas. Also, I was still asserting my independence, and it was a little close to home. The University of Texas was a large medical school that had been around for a long time, and Texas Tech wasn't nearly as old and as well established. Same thing with Texas A&M.

I interviewed at all the schools. When I interviewed at Texas Tech, I was interviewed by a PhD and two MDs.

My third interview was with an OB/GYN doctor. He looked through my record, and I sat there waiting for him to start asking me questions. He looked up and said, "Ronny Jackson, I think the last time I saw you, I was spanking your butt!" It turned out he had been the OB/GYN doctor who had delivered me when I was born. His name was Dr. Ansley, and he was my mom's OB/GYN doctor for almost thirty years. He saw my mom and dad's name on my application and quickly realized he had taken care of my mom all those years and actually delivered me. Wow, what an icebreaker!

I don't think my dad changed his mind and decided that going to college was a good idea until I graduated from med school. My parents were excited and proud when I got into med school, but I don't think the significance of it sunk in until I graduated. I think that on the day I graduated from med school, my dad might have thought, *Wow, this turned out to be a good idea after all,* but before that, my dad just thought that it was mostly a waste of time.

When my parents came to my graduation at the University of Texas, and I walked across that stage as Dr. Ronny Jackson, that was the day they realized I had finally made something out of all of this.

2.

I was really excited when I finally got accepted to my number one choice at the University of Texas Medical Branch in Galveston. I specifically wanted to go there because I had already been living there while attending Texas A&M, my girlfriend and future wife was there, and most of my friends were also there.

I applied to the army scholarship, the navy scholarship, and the air force scholarship. I never heard back from the air force; I guess I wasn't meant to "Fly High." I received the army scholarship and navy scholarship.

I had to decide which one of those I wanted, and I figured, I'm a marine biology major, I attended Texas A&M at Galveston, I love diving and the water, I like being on the coast. I didn't want to end up in the army, where I would be trapped inland somewhere. The navy definitely had the coolest bases, and there was a good chance I would be stationed somewhere on the coast.

So, I decided on the navy scholarship and got it. They paid for four years of my medical school, and I owed them four years in return.

They paid for my books, tuition, and fees and gave me a small stipend to live on, which was great.

I didn't even end up spending all the money they gave me. I had a couple of hundred dollars a month extra that went straight into my savings account. So, while all my classmates finished four years of medical school and were a couple hundred thousand dollars in debt, I got out of med school and had money in the bank.

My commitment to the navy was for four years, and I thought I would give them those four years back and get out. I figured I'd be an emergency medicine doctor somewhere in Texas, make a lot of money, live in a big house, and so on and so forth, but it didn't work out that way.

Instead, I loved it! One of the things that hooked me was, as soon as I got in, I found out about this program they have called the Diving Medical Officer Program, where you can be both a navy deep-sea diver and a doctor. A diver and a doctor? That was tailor-made for me. I was a marine biology major, a scuba diver, and had just finished medical school, and I could do both? Sign me up!

Before I could do anything, I had to do my internship year, or my first year of residency. Everybody must do that in order to take the third and final part of their licensing exam and become licensed to practice independently. After that, you have a few options in the navy. You can continue with the residency of your choice, not do a residency and practice as a general medical officer, or you can defer the remainder of your residency for a few years and train as a diving medical officer or flight surgeon. I chose diving medicine.

As soon as I graduated from medical school, I was recommissioned on active duty as a lieutenant, and Jane and I packed up and headed to our first duty station in Portsmouth, Virginia, to start my internship.

Jane was nine months pregnant when we relocated, and I knew that she was going to deliver sometime shortly after we got there. As an intern, I had to do rotations in all the specialty areas, such as emergency medicine, pediatrics, internal medicine, general surgery, psychiatry, and OB/GYN. Since Jane was about to deliver any day, I asked for OB/GYN to be my first rotation. I figured that would make it easier for me to be there when the baby was born.

As soon as we got there, I had a couple of weeks of orientation, and I made a special effort to meet as many of the residents and staff in the obstetrics department as I could. The following week I showed up for my first day at work. My first day as a practicing physician. The entire first week was crazy. I worked eighteen hours a day. During that first week, I came home one morning after working twenty-six hours straight. I hadn't slept at all the night before; I was super tired and physically completely spent. When I got home, Jane was outside, nine months pregnant, and she was mowing the yard. I went inside and was planning to go straight to bed.

She came in all sweaty from mowing, and she said, "My water broke," and I said, "You gotta be kidding me." She said, "No."

I thought, *There's no way I can go back up there right now; I have to get some sleep.* So, I told her, "I'm going to go to the back room, I'm going to sleep for three hours, you wake me up in three hours, and I'll take you to the hospital."

She said, "Are you kidding me? My water broke."

"You're fine," I said. "It's your first baby; nothing's going to happen for a while. Just give me three hours; I've got to sleep for three hours."

I slept for three hours, and she woke me up, and we went back to the hospital.

The nurses were getting her all settled in, and the chief resident came in to check her out and say hi. Luckily, I had spent a little time with him during the two weeks of orientation. He talked to Jane for a few minutes, and then he turned to me and said, "Are you going to do this or are we going to do this?"

I said, "I'm okay doing it, but if something goes wrong, if there's any damage or if she needs to be sewn up, I need you guys to do that. I'm the new guy, I don't want that responsibility! But otherwise, yes, I got it."

And he said, "Okay, it's all yours."

So, I went right to work. I got in there, and about twelve hours later, I delivered my daughter, Libby. The first baby I had ever delivered as a doctor and the first baby I ever delivered in the United States Navy was my own daughter. I've delivered close to a hundred babies since then, but she was the very first. It just worked out perfectly, and being blessed with the opportunity to deliver my daughter was a great way to start my intern year.

Jane might tell you that I was very formal about it, more business-like than I should have been as the baby's father. Maybe? But I had the responsibility and definitely didn't want to mess this one up. I'll admit I was very professionally focused, and my priority until Libby was delivered and everything else was finished was getting the job done. I made sure everything was good to go before she started pushing and the baby started coming out. Once the baby started coming out, I was focused, and I delivered the baby a lot faster and easier than I expected.

Jane pushed hard five or six times, and Libby was delivered. I immediately passed her to the nurse, cut the umbilical cord, and went right back to focusing on the next step, which was delivering the placenta. The nurse wrapped Libby up and passed her to Jane at the head of the bed. I delivered the placenta and checked to make sure there was no bleeding. Then I was done.

After that, I took a step back and transitioned from being the doctor who delivered the baby to being Libby's dad. Later, I would also deliver my third child, Matt, at the same hospital in Portsmouth, Virginia.

During that very busy intern year in Portsmouth, I also took the next step in my career and applied for the Undersea Medical Officer Program. I got accepted to the program, and as soon as I finished my intern year, they sent me straight to Groton, Connecticut, for submarine school and then Panama City, Florida, for dive school. I completed a total of six months of training in submarine medicine, diving medicine, and operational diving. I became a fully qualified navy deep-sea diver and undersea medical officer uniquely trained in submarine and diving medicine.

I was now a physician, but I was also a full-blown navy deep-sea diver, walking around on the bottom of the ocean with a helmet and a hose. I was qualified in every diving rig the navy had; MK 20/21 surface supply, scuba, and rebreathers such as MK 16 and LAR 5. I was living the dream.

Through hard work and effort, I finished with honors. I had the highest GPA and the highest physical scores in my entire dive class. The tradition is, if you're the honor man, they lay all the billets or available assignments out there, and you get your first choice, and then everybody else gets whatever the detailer decides to give to them.

I chose the only job that was offered to our class that was a true diving billet and not on a submarine or ship. I took the assignment as an instructor at the Naval Diving and Salvage Training Center in Panama City Beach, Florida. I was hoping for an operational diving job with the SEAL Team or an explosive ordnance disposal unit, but there were none open when my class graduated. It wasn't exactly what I wanted, but it was the best billet in my class, and it turned out to be a real blessing in disguise. So, Jane and I packed up and moved to Florida.

I should note, however, that Jane had just delivered our second child, Ben, about twelve weeks prior. In the middle of my undersea medical officer training, the day before I made the transition from Groton, Connecticut, to Panama City, Florida, to begin the deep-sea diving part of my training, Jane went into labor. I, of course, wanted to be the one to deliver him, but her doctor in Groton was not military. He was a civilian, and because we had not been there long, I had only met him once or twice. Since my credentialing didn't extend beyond the military, and I didn't really have a relationship with this guy, I had to let him do it. Everything went well, but we had to leave the next day to head to Florida and continue my training. So, I loaded Jane, my one-year-old daughter, and my one-day-old son in the van, and we headed that way. We drove for a while but stopped in Silver Spring, Maryland, where Jane's mother and sister lived, and I dropped Jane and the rest of the family off there. Driving all the way to Florida and being all by herself with a newborn and a one-year-old would not have been any fun, so she stayed there while I continued.

As I mentioned above, once my training was done, I ended up getting assigned in Florida, and Jane and the family joined me then. While assigned to the dive school in Florida, I got to do lots of really cool stuff other than teach diving and diving medicine. I spent a lot of time supporting the US Army's Twentieth Special Forces Group, and as a result, they sent me to jump school in Fort Benning, Georgia. I jumped every opportunity I got after that and got lots of jumps in with the Army Special Forces, the Marines, the Navy SEALS, and Navy EOD. The navy also sent me to Hawaii, where I was assigned temporarily to the SEAL Delivery Team (SDV-1) and spent a few months operating from submarines with the SEALs. There are few things cooler than locking out of a submarine. I was initially aboard the USS *Kamehameha*, which was an old Benjamin Franklin-class ballistic missile submarine. It had been converted into a SEAL delivery platform. We would crawl up through one of the old vertical missile tubes and into a dry deck shelter attached to the top of the submarine that houses the SEAL delivery vehicle. Then the dry deck shelter would begin to flood. The first time you do it, it's crazy. You are sitting there in nothing but your dive shorts and dive boots with a mask around your neck, and the water starts rising. Eventually, it gets to your head, and you put your mask on and grab a regulator hanging from the ceiling. The pressure equalizes, and the door pops open. You can then swim about freely. The first time I did it, I swam out and positioned myself in the concave part of the open door in order to stay out of the way. As I swam out, I grabbed the top of the shelter and pulled myself up. It was incredible because the visibility in Hawaii is awesome. When I looked back over the top of the shelter, I could feel the water going through my hair, and I could see the sail of the submarine. At that point, I realized I wasn't attached to anything, and I was literally underwater, hanging on to the front of a ballistic missile submarine! Pretty crazy.

I spent a lot of time on different submarines while in Hawaii and completed all my submarine warfare qualifications in the process. I ultimately earned my submarine warfare designation and was awarded my medical submarine dolphins insignia. This was in addition to the deep-sea diving insignia and the jump wings I had already earned and was currently wearing.

About two years into being an instructor at the dive school in Florida, a job opened with Explosive Ordnance Disposal Mobile Unit Eight (EODMU 8) in Sicily. This was the opportunity I had been waiting for, and I jumped all over it. Jane and I were off to Sicily!

We chose not to live on base or in areas where most of the Americans assigned to the area lived. Instead, we moved to a town called Mascalucia, and I bought a little Alfa Romeo that I could get back and forth to work in. We rented a house in the middle of an orchard that was full of nothing but orange, lemon, and olive trees, and it was huge. It was located about halfway up Mount Etna, which was an active volcano.

Every now and then, the volcano would erupt, and massive black plumes of smoke would pour out of the top. You could sit on our back porch and watch lava run down the side of the mountain. I would get up in the morning—sometimes, it would still be dark as I walked out of the house to my car. I would hear a strange noise in the trees, and the first time I heard it, I didn't know what it was. When I got to my car, I figured it out. It was tiny lava rocks raining down into the trees. The windshield of my car was covered with these tiny rocks.

It was such a great place, and the people were some of the friendliest you will ever meet. They were just like people from West Texas. They welcomed us to sit at their table and have dinner with them. Your kids could run all over the restaurant completely unsupervised;

people would let them sit down at their table and eat with them, and they didn't know them at all.

They were accustomed to Americans being around because of the big military base there: Sigonella Naval Air Station, which was down at the bottom of the mountain. I think they appreciated that we kind of adopted their culture and didn't live down in base housing with everybody else in the military. Instead, we embraced the experience and lived in a community with the locals.

While stationed in Sicily, I was one of the junior officers in charge of a deployable detachment, so I traveled all over the world. I was gone maybe nine months out of the year. Jane would be home with the kids, and I'd be traveling all over Europe, Africa, and the Middle East, leading diving exercises and operations.

The hard part was being away from my kids. Because they were so young, it really felt like I had missed a lot when I returned. My wife got it; she grew up as an army brat. Her dad was an army cardiothoracic surgeon who was on active duty for twenty-eight years, including two tours in Vietnam. She knew when we got married what it was going to be like as a military family.

She was super supportive and did a bunch of traveling on her own too. She took the kids and went all over Italy and the rest of Europe. They definitely made the most of it and really took advantage of the opportunity and the history all around us. She loved everything about living in Italy, especially the people, the food, the culture, and the opportunity to travel.

Life couldn't get much better for me. Every day, I was jumping out of airplanes, fast-roping out of helicopters, blowing stuff up, shooting all kinds of weapons. I loved the operational side of my job. We'd cast out of helicopters into the Mediterranean or the Adriatic Sea, climb into small boats, run ashore, set up camp, break out a bunch of C-4 explosives, and blow things up. It was every ten-year-old boy's dream.

In addition, the travel was incredible. We were doing what we call engagement exercises with various NATO countries and countries that wanted to be members of NATO. We would fly to Norway, Albania, Estonia, Latvia, Slovenia, Italy, Germany, and others. We would train their divers on how to work with the Americans and teach them about operations, equipment, and tactics involving diving and underwater bomb recovery and disposal. We also did lots of real-world operations around the world, diving on live ordnance, and I was an active part of that as well. At one point, I had found more underwater ordnance than any diver in my unit.

Working with these NATO and prospective NATO countries was great. They all received a significant amount of money from the United States, and they wanted to make sure it continued. As a result, they were falling all over themselves to make a good impression. They took us to some incredibly unique and exotic places to dive, and we were rock stars no matter where we went. They really rolled out the red carpet. It was lots of fun, and I learned to appreciate the many cultures represented. Looking back, it was really an important time in my professional growth.

People would ask me all the time, "When will you get out of the military and get back into the civilian world and start making some money?" I would say to them, "I will go back to the civilian world when the navy assigns me a normal boring job." At the time, and essentially the entire time I was in the navy, I was doing things that could not be replicated in the civilian world and things that money could not buy. I had no intention of getting out any time soon.

I ultimately wanted to be an emergency medicine doctor. I had planned to be a diving medical officer for a couple of years then apply to finish my residency in emergency medicine. However, I was having too much fun with my operational job as a diving medical officer and deferred residency longer than I planned. I was about five years out from finishing my internship now. I knew that if I wanted to continue to be promoted and move up the ranks in the military, I would have to get board certified in a medical specialty. I didn't want to leave what I was doing and go back to residency, but it was obvious that was what I had to do. I was a lieutenant at the time, and I would not be promoted to lieutenant commander without becoming board certified in emergency medicine.

So, I applied for the emergency medicine program at the Naval Hospital in Portsmouth, Virginia. I was accepted, Jane and I packed up the family, and we moved back to the States. My first day of residency was on September 1, 2001. I regretted leaving my operational command in Italy, but not near as bad as I would a little over a week later when the attacks of September 11 took place.

3.

On September 11, we were in the middle of our second week of new resident orientation. All the residents were in a classroom in the emergency department. We were going over just real basic stuff, and they were telling us what our schedules and rotations would look like, as well as some of the administrative tasks and academic requirements we had to complete. I was on a break and getting a cup of coffee.

I was walking back from the coffee shop in the hospital and walked past the dermatology clinic and just happened to look over and see the images on the TV.

I wasn't sure what I was looking at. *What is that? I can see smoke coming out of the World Trade Center.*

I read the ticker at the bottom of the screen saying that a plane had hit the building. Initially, I thought that an aircraft had accidentally hit the building. I figured it was a small plane that had inadvertently run into the building and set a few of the offices on fire. This was right after it happened, and there was quite a bit of smoke, and initially, that is all I saw.

I stood there for a minute, watching it from the hall and not able to hear what was being said. Then I saw the replay of an actual 747 going into the building! I thought, *What the hell is going on here? Oh my gosh, that's no accident.* I stood there frozen, watching what was happening. A few minutes later, I saw the second plane hit the building and instantly knew it had been intentional and that we were under attack!

I went back to the classroom and everybody was talking about what was going on. Then the residency program director walked in and said, "We don't know what's going on, but a plane just hit the World Trade Center." After that, we had reports that the Pentagon had been hit, and at that point, the program director said, "You guys go home; check on your family. More important things are going on today than going through this orientation," and he dismissed us all. We all immediately understood the seriousness and the implications of this act on each and every one of us as active-duty military members.

That day was horrible. Every bone in my body was telling me to go straight back to my unit and get in this fight I knew was about to take place. I knew that my previous unit would be a part of the response, and I felt sick that I was no longer there.

A lot of us knew that we were probably going to war in some form or fashion. It quickly was reported that it had been a terrorist attack, and perhaps Osama bin Laden was involved. I didn't realize then that it would be the beginning of a war that would last for decades.

My kids were still young in 2001. My youngest hadn't been born yet, and my two oldest were five and six. I tried to explain to them in terms a five-year-old would understand that some evil people had attacked the Pentagon and the World Trade Center. It was, of course, many years later before they realized what had actually happened and how it forever changed the world we all live in.

One thing I knew for sure, I knew damn well that President Bush was going to do something about it. I didn't know him personally at that point, but I had seen him on TV and the way he reacted that day to what had happened. I knew that he wouldn't let it go; there was going to be hell to pay.

They were going to find out who did it; those people were going to pay the price. But honestly, I was very eager to be a part of retaliating, of exacting some revenge on the people who had done this. I didn't know what our response as a nation and as the military would be, but I figured it would quickly evolve beyond sending a few tomahawk missiles somewhere and would involve troops on the ground.

My old team was already getting their gear together in anticipation. They were a forward-deployed explosive ordnance disposal team; they worked closely every day with special operations, with both the Navy SEALs and the Army Special Forces. I knew for a fact that, based on the units that they worked with, they would be among the very first people to respond to something like this.

I was at the point where I was begging my residency program director to let me out of the program. I told him I wanted to defer for a year to go back to Italy and deploy with my previous unit. We were about to go to war, and I wanted in!

However, it quickly became apparent that that wasn't going to happen. The navy had already recategorized me as "in training." They weren't going to let me leave until I was done. They made this point to many of us because I wasn't the only one who wanted to defer training and get in the fight.

Our program director explained to all of us that what we needed to do right now was focus on becoming the best emergency medicine doctors we could be and that each of us would get our chance to make a difference. Man, was he ever right! For the next ten years, almost every physician graduating from the program went to war in the Middle East in response to what happened on 9/11.

The United States Marine Corps cannot fight without Navy Medicine, and navy emergency medicine physicians are on the tip of that spear. The new norm was accepted, that if you were a board-certified navy emergency medicine physician, you belonged to the Marine Corps!

I accepted my fate as a resident for the next few years. I just sucked it up. I worked hard for the next three years to become the best emergency medicine doctor I could be.

Three years later, I graduated, and the war was still going on. In fact, it just kept growing and getting more and more ramped up throughout my residency.

By the time I graduated, I had made it clear to everybody that the first thing I wanted to do, the second I got out, was to deploy to Iraq or Afghanistan. The navy honored my request and sent me right to Camp Lejeune, where I joined the Second Marines and went straight to Iraq.

This was a good fit for me. I wanted to go where marines were fighting on the front lines. This is what I was trained to do. I had an operational background supporting tactical units like EOD, SEALS, and special operations, and now, I was a specialist in emergency medicine and battlefield trauma. Marines were giving life and limb, and I wanted to be there to do my part and make sure these heroes made it home to their families.

I deployed with a Surgical Shock Trauma Platoon (S/STP) assigned to Second Marines, Combat Logistics Regiment 25. I was the officer in charge of the resuscitation and emergency medicine part of this team. We were a relatively small team made up of surgeons, nurses, and corpsmen. We worked out of tents and were right on the battlefield at a place called Taqaddum, which is located between Fallujah and Ramadi. The nickname of the base was TQ, and it was an old Iraqi airbase.

We were very busy. The marines would leave the base every day and go into Ramadi and surrounding small towns to clear houses and hunt down the insurgents. Every day, they would be attacked with small arms fire, RPGs, and IEDs. The injuries we received almost every day were horrible. Marines, soldiers, and sailors were being delivered to our triage pad directly from tactical vehicles and helicopters. We were getting them straight from the battle within minutes of injury. They were arriving with missing limbs, bowels hanging out of their abdomen, grey matter protruding from their head, and with horrible burns and bleeding.

Simultaneously on some occasions, the enemy would launch rockets and mortars into our base while we were actively working on casualties. I was struck at how similar the situation I found myself in was to an episode of the TV show I watched growing up called *M*A*S*H*. First, we were working out of tents with patients on canvas litters. We were dressed in cammies and combat boots, and most of us were armed. We would be operating on patients, and there would be lots of activity with nurses and corpsmen calling for medications, blood, and other supplies. Everybody was totally focused on their task in trying to save these casualties, and all of a sudden, there would be a loud crack as a 122 mm rocket landed a couple of hundred yards away. There was then instantly a brief period where everyone froze, and it was silent. Then everyone went right back to what they were doing, and the noise resumed. You could smell the scent of gunpowder briefly passing through the tent. I even noticed dust falling from the lights over the patients once after a rocket hit. It was just like an episode of *M*A*S*H*. That show was about the Korean War, and here we were in 2005, in the same setting and same situation.

We carried a gun and wore body armor everywhere we went. We never knew when they were going to fire rockets or mortars at us, and occasionally, they even shot at us from outside the base with small arms. As a matter of fact, I used to run every day, and eventually, I had to change my running route because there was a section of the route where the enemy would take shots at us. I didn't wear a pistol or body armor when I was running, but that was the only exception. Even when I was operating on patients, I had a sidearm strapped to my leg.

We did everything we could to save as many people as possible. We had an incredible record and kept most of them alive. But of course, some died, and there was nothing we could do about that. We'd work on our patients for hours, opening their chest, then their abdomen, then their pelvis, trying to find every source of bleeding and stop it. Most of our casualties had many injuries with multiple fragments from an IED having torn through their bodies with multiple sources of bleeding. We had a "walking blood bank" that we called on frequently. Some patients would need ten, twenty, even thirty units of blood. We could not keep that much blood on hand. We would send a message out over the base comms system asking everyone with the type of blood we needed to come to the S/STP immediately. Marines would line up everywhere to give blood to their wounded teammates. We would take blood from a marine or soldier and, a few minutes later, give it to another one.

I had been an emergency medicine physician for a while prior to arriving in Iraq, so I had seen plenty of patients die in the hospital. Often, I was also the one who had to break the news to their families about their deaths, and I understood how devastating that news is to a family. Emotionally and psychologically, I was accustomed to and prepared for death. Dealing with it was my job. Despite that, it's different in war—especially the first time it happens. It's still difficult, but I remember the very first time that it happened; it hit me and my team hard.

He was a young marine, just a kid about twenty, twenty-one years old, and he had been hit by an IED that had been buried in the road just a mile away from our field hospital. He was badly injured and had fragments from the IED in his chest, his abdomen, his face, arms, and legs. He was awake and alert but bleeding internally, so we knew we had to act quickly. Young, healthy, physically fit kids his age have incredible reserves and can look like they are doing much better than they actually are. They can be hemodynamically stable; their blood pressure and pulse can look pretty good until they get to a critical point, and then it just drops off all at once.

This kid came in, and he was a little tachycardic (rapid pulse), but his blood pressure was okay. He had blood coming from several areas on his lower chest, his abdomen, and his back. We knew right away he was going straight to the surgical tent, where they could open his abdomen and figure out what his injuries were. I was getting him ready for surgery. I was putting a central IV into his neck and preparing to put him to sleep and intubate him. He was still awake and looked pretty good, considering. There were five or six of us around him, cutting his clothes off, placing monitors on his body, and getting him ready for surgery. There was a lot of noise and activity. I was trying to talk to him as I was working since I could tell he was scared and needed some reassurance. I distinctly remember he said to me, "Hey, Doc, am I going to be okay?"

I said, "You're going to be fine. Don't you worry about it. I'm going to take great care of you."

I was at the head of the bed, helping the anesthesiologist. The nurse verified the medications with me and then pushed them into his IV in order to paralyze him and put him to sleep. He was looking at me when the drugs kicked in and he became sedated and stopped breathing. At that point, I placed the endotracheal tube in his airway, and we put him on the ventilator for the surgery. I stayed at the head of the bed and managed his airway and pushed the fluids, medications, and blood into the IVs as needed. The surgeon opened his abdomen up, and this kid just started bleeding like crazy. I mean, his abdomen was full of blood; we would suction it out, and it would just start coming up from everywhere. We continued to suction the blood out and pack the area with surgical gauze in order to stop the bleeding and see where it was coming from. It turns out the fragments from the IED had torn through his pelvis and lacerated multiple large veins and small arteries.

He had been mostly stable, but now that he was losing large amounts of blood, his pulse started going through the roof, and his blood pressure started dropping. We started transfusing him with as much blood as we could. We had activated the walking blood bank, and lots of his fellow marines lined up to give blood to save his life.

The surgeons were working frantically to control his bleeding and even went so far as to open his chest up and cross-clamp his descending aorta. Everyone was working as hard as they could. I was at the head of the bed and trying to cram as much blood into his body as possible and as fast as I could. I remember I was physically squeezing the bags with my hands and began to get cramps in my forearms. We gave this kid over thirty units of blood and worked on him for almost three hours. Everyone involved gave 110 percent. He died.

It was devastating for my team, and you could tell it just sucked the life out of everybody in the room. I just felt horrible. I couldn't stop thinking about how his parents had said bye to him, not knowing they would never speak to him again. I felt guilty that I had been the last person he talked to and that the last thing I had told him was he was going to be okay. Now he was lying here in front of me, dead. Only twenty years old.

That stuck with me for a while. I remember I got the team together that night to talk about what was going on and make sure everybody was okay. Some of the nurses were crying. It was the first patient we had lost, and it was a dramatic one. I mean, the way he came in, everybody thought he would be okay, and instead, he died on our watch. That was the first of many horribly injured marines and soldiers we would see, and unfortunately, not the last we would watch die.

I also had the unenviable duty of being the mortuary affairs officer, which probably had more of an impact on me than anything I have ever done. This meant that every time someone was killed in combat, I had to examine the body and sign the death certificate before the family could be notified and the body could be sent home. I have seen up close what it means to sacrifice everything for this country, and that is just one reason why I am so disgusted by what is going on in our country and in our military right now.

Anyone killed in our area of responsibility would come to TQ, the base I lived on. The body would go straight to our morgue, which was located about a mile and a half from the tent that I lived in. I had a radio, and I would get calls at like three o'clock in the morning to come to the morgue, that there was a body coming in. I would have to get up, put on my gun, put on my body armor, put on my helmet, get on my Gator, and drive down to the morgue. I would then examine the body, determine the cause of death, and sign the death certificate.

Nothing could happen until I did that. I'd go in, and there'd be a body bag. I would unzip it, look inside, and honestly sometimes couldn't tell which end was the head and which was the feet. It was just a bag of hamburger meat with bone shards sticking up out of it, blown up and burnt. I would have guys that were literally burnt to a crisp, missing their limbs, or, on one occasion, their head. A couple of times, there would be nothing but a five-gallon bucket on the ground with some body parts in it, because that was all they'd recovered. Most of the time, when I signed the person's death certificate, I would just put down something like, "total body dismemberment status post-IED." At that point, the body could be flown back to Dover and reunited with the family. That was my job. It was a gruesome duty. It was the job nobody else wanted for obvious reasons.

No one wants to see a young man die, or be tragically injured, dismembered, or with a devastating traumatic brain injury. Those who survive go back to the States and are never the same. It's hard to describe what it is like when you see a young guy come in at twenty years old with his legs blown off and genitals gone. It is hard to stop thinking about all that person has lost for the rest of their life. I have also been there when they wake up, and you have to help them understand the extent of their injuries and how messed up they are.

They don't always get it right away. Many of them are devastated and immediately destroyed; some of them are in denial initially. I will say, I had the fortune of seeing many of these same guys years later at Walter Reed National Military Medical Center and could not have been any prouder or more inspired. Most were there after years of physical and mental rehabilitation, many surgeries, and most had at least one prosthetic limb. The attitude and the positive outlook on life that these men had were unbelievable. Despite all they had given up and sacrificed for their country, none of them dwelled on what they had lost. They all looked ahead, and all saw their future as bright. All were proud of their service and had few regrets. Their bodies were broken, but their souls were indestructible. They were, and still are, an inspiration and make me proud to be an American.

As for me, when I first arrived in Iraq, I said to myself, "Oh, my God, what have I gotten myself into?" I was a junior emergency medicine physician and all by myself. I was taking over for two very senior emergency medicine physicians who had been there for almost a year. I was really worried I may have bitten off more than I could chew. However, what I realized quickly was that I was well trained and knew what I was doing, and a lot of it was instinct for me. I would stick to the basics, rely on my training, and work my way through the process.

By the time I left the battlefield in Iraq, my confidence in my abilities was through the roof. I went back to the United States and back to work in the emergency department, and I thought to myself, *I don't care what comes through that door; there is nothing that can fluster me.* I felt like I had seen it all, done it all, and that there was nothing I couldn't deal with.

4.

One day, while I was still deployed in Iraq, I checked my old email account from the Naval Medical Center in Portsmouth, where I had been assigned before coming to Iraq. When I opened it up, I saw an email from my detailer. My detailer is the person who decides, every two or three years, where I live and what job I have in the navy. The email said, "You've been selected to apply for a job at the White House as the White House physician." I thought, *What? How did this happen? What is all this about?* I had heard about this job in passing but didn't know anything about it and certainly never imagined being considered for it. It turns out that my department head, Captain Joel Roos, at the hospital I had just left, heard the White House was looking for an emergency medicine doctor and he nominated me, without my even knowing about it. I was surprised, a little confused, but excited. The email from my detailer went on to say, "Please have your CV, personal statement, last six performance reports, security information, official photo…" The email continued with a mile-long list of other requirements.

By the time I saw it, it had already been sitting in my inbox for over a week, and I had five days to get everything in. I thought to myself, *There's no way I can do this. I'm out here in Iraq in the middle of nowhere; there's just no way I can make this happen.*

Initially, I decided I wasn't even going to waste my time with it. But that night, I called and talked to my wife, and she said, "Well, what are you going to do?"

"There's no way I can get all of this put together and turned in before the deadline while I am out here in the middle of the desert," I said.

"Well, Ronny, you should go ahead and give it a shot."

"Jane, I can't put together a competitive package out here, and it will just be a waste of time."

She made the case that it wouldn't be a waste of time, and if I didn't get the job, it still might make a difference down the road with another opportunity. It might set me apart from my peers if I was able to say I applied and was considered for the job of White House physician.

So I followed Jane's advice and scrambled to get everything done as fast as possible. Nothing was easy, and it wasn't near as clean and professional as I would have wanted it to be. Instead of an official photo in the proper uniform, I had my picture taken with my cammies on in front of the blast barriers. I was doing my best to electronically generate the documents they needed, despite not even having ready access to a computer and no access to all the historical information needed for my clearance documents. Jane was digging stuff out of the filing cabinet at home and trying to fax it in, and the hospital in Portsmouth was jumping through hoops to get all my credentialing information updated and sent to them.

I figured all the other applicants would have a nice, "squared away," perfectly organized package, and I was going to have this big pile of garbage, and I didn't have a snowball's chance in hell of being selected. But Jane and I were a great team, and I got it all in by the deadline.

A couple of months went by; I didn't hear anything about it, not a word. I called the detailer to try and find out what was going on. He said, "I don't know, I don't have any oversight of it; it's really up to the White House at this point. I don't know what they're doing with it, and I haven't heard anything." I thought to myself, *Well, somebody probably already got the job; I just don't know about it because I'm out here in the middle of nowhere.*

Well, checking your email in the middle of a combat zone in the desert is not easy. So, assuming I didn't make the cut, I gradually went back to the previous practice of just checking that old email account every week or so. Then one day, about two and a half months into this whole process, I logged on to the account, and there was an email from my detailer saying, "You've been selected as one of three people to interview for a job at the White House. Please be in Washington, DC, in five days." I was like, *Holy crap, five days? Are you kidding me? There's no way, right?* I was excited that I had made it that far, but I had the instant realization that this was where the road ended because there was no way I could be in DC in five days.

I tell people that sometimes the great opportunities in life are based on being in the right place at the right time. More importantly, sometimes it's about having a few good people around you who want to see you succeed, who are in a position to help you, and who invest in your success even though they have nothing personally to gain from it. Sometimes it is a combination of the two. That was the case for me. It turned out that the commanding general for all of the marines in Iraq used to be the military aide for President George H. W. Bush, Bush Senior. This is the guy who follows the president around everywhere he goes and carries the "nuclear football." The other guy who follows the president around everywhere he goes is the White House physician. These two people are together and just steps away from the president twenty-four seven, 365 days a year. So the general had worked closely with the White House physician for a couple of years when he was at the White House. He knew exactly what the job entailed. He knew what was being asked of me, even though I didn't. He knew it was a unique opportunity that I would probably never get again, and he wanted to make sure I was able to take full advantage of this opportunity.

At the time, I didn't know the general that well. He had come to our trauma tent a few times when we were receiving casualties, and I knew who he was and had said hi to him in passing, but I didn't know him personally.

I had told my boss, who had told his boss, who told the general about the offer to interview for the job. When the general heard about it, he summoned me to his office. I sat down, and he said, "Tell me what's going on." I went through the whole story with him, and he said, "What are you going to do?"

I said, "Well, sir, there's no way I'm going to be in DC in five days." I explained that I was going to see if I could do a video teleconference or maybe a telephone interview. I didn't know how competitive I was going to be, but I would give it my best shot.

Immediately, he picked the phone up and called the air boss, the person who controls all the air assets in the entire theater. He talked to him for a few minutes, and the last thing he said to him was, "I want his ass out of here by sunset," and he hung up the phone. He looked at me and said, "Go pack your bag; you're leaving."

And, of course, my reply was, "Yes, sir."

I went back to the tiny one-room plywood shack I lived in with seven other guys, threw a few things into my seabag, went out to the flight line, got on a helicopter, and flew to Baghdad. Once in Baghdad, I got on a C-5 cargo plane full of broken helicopters; flew back to Cherry Point, North Carolina; got a rental car; and drove back to Virginia Beach, where my family and I were living.

I was in a panic. I was supposed to be in DC the next day, interviewing for this job, and I was supposed to interview two days in a business suit and one day in a uniform. But while in Iraq, I had been running six to ten miles a day the whole time I had been there, and I had lost forty pounds. I had no clothes that fit. None.

In a desperate move, my wife and I went straight to Men's Wearhouse. I bought a new suit, and I gave them my sob story and begged them to tailor it on the spot. Luckily, they felt sorry for me and were able to get it done. They even fixed up my uniform and made it acceptable. Once that was done, I got back in my rental car, drove to DC, made it to the White House, and interviewed for the job for three days.

At the end of the three days, they told me I had gotten the job. I went back to Iraq to finish the four months left on my tour, and then I essentially came straight from Iraq to the White House. That was in early 2006. Little did I know that I'd be spending the next fourteen years there.

Interviewing for a job at the White House was an interesting process. I didn't know it at the time, but it was a process I would be overseeing for many years. The three-day process is made up of multiple interviews. You interview with a small group, a large group, in a formal setting, in an informal setting, and participate in after-hours socials. You spend a whole day just going through nothing but security and background investigations. Security professionals have already amassed a large file on you by the time you arrive and then interview you relentlessly regarding everything imaginable in your background. All necessary to get a top-secret, SCI, Yankee White clearance that allows you to work one on one with the president of the United States. They, of course, spend a lot of time also making sure you have the medical skills and operational background needed. Everybody in the White House Medical Unit gets a vote on whether they want you there.

During the social gatherings, you eat and have the opportunity to have a few drinks and get to know everyone a little better. It's also an opportunity to find out who can remain professional in that setting and who will have too much to drink and be a potential embarrassment to the unit down the road. More than a few have wrecked their chances of working at the White House because of the social.

My selection was one of the more legendary ones. It was kind of crazy because I wasn't the primary pick for the job. There were three of us who interviewed for the same position, and they had originally picked somebody else; I was the alternate. But the guy they picked had something happen with his family, and he backed out as soon as they told him he had the job.

When we left that third day before they announced the results, they told us, "Okay, you guys can go home; we will call you tomorrow morning and let you know what we decide." I went back to my hotel in DC, and I thought, *Well, I'm not going to leave until I hear from them; I don't want to be on the road when they call.* So, I stayed as late as

I possibly could, got a late checkout, and waited for them to contact me. They didn't, and eventually I had to check out of the hotel and drive back to Virginia and start getting ready to return to Iraq as soon as possible. I figured it was bad news and they had selected one of the other guys.

Later that evening, back at home in Virginia Beach, I finally got a phone call from the White House Medical Unit director, and he said, "Congratulations, you got the job." I was super excited! He spent the next five minutes talking to me about the job requirements and what the next steps were.

I said thank you and that I was scheduled to fly back to Iraq tomorrow but was looking forward to joining the team as soon as I returned. He said, "Woah, wait, is this Ronny? Ronny, I am so sorry—I thought I was talking to Art." Then he said, "Ronny, I'm sorry…you didn't get the job. Art got the job. I thought I was talking to Art. I called the wrong number."

"Are you kidding me?" I responded.

"Well, if it makes you feel any better, Ronny," he said, "you were the alternate. It was a tough decision, and we went back and forth, back and forth. It fell to a one-vote margin, and Art ended up getting it."

I thanked him for his time and consideration. My mom and dad just happened to be there because they had come up to Virginia Beach for an early Christmas with my family. My mom, my dad, Jane, and my kids had been desperately waiting with me, wondering if I got the job or not. When the director first told me I had, I'd given them a thumbs up, and they were all excited.

I hung up the phone, and my parents said, "You got the job?" I said, "No." They were confused, because listening to my side of the phone call, it had sounded like I got the job. Everyone wanted to know what happened.

"I didn't get the job," I said. "I don't want to talk about it right now." I was disappointed about it and walked off.

Then, within five minutes, the phone rang again. "Hey, Ronny, this is the director again. I can't believe I'm calling you right back to say this, but if you still want that job, it's yours."

"What?" I asked.

"Well, I just called Art, and he backed down. He said he couldn't take the job because of a family issue; his wife's not on board. The job is yours if you want it."

I said, "Sure." I thought to myself, *This guy tells me I got the job, then he tells me I don't have the job, then he calls me back and tells me I got the job. Is this part of the interview process?* Maybe this was a test designed to see how you reacted to something like that. Turns out it wasn't, but it was definitely high drama.

My parents were excited. They loved George Bush, so they were fired up that I was going to work for him and his administration. It was a big deal in my community too. Everybody was thrilled about it, including me. It was going to be fun! I wasn't the first emergency medicine doctor at the White House; there had been a couple before me, but they didn't stay long. So I would be the only emergency medicine doctor on the staff, and I eventually became the first emergency medicine doctor to ever be appointed as physician to the president.

The White House wanted me to start right away. They said, "We can have the navy backfill you in Iraq. You don't need to go back; we can bring you on board right away." But I didn't want someone to be taken from their family and sent into harm's way to complete my tour because I ended up with a great opportunity. So, I told them that I was going back. I needed to finish my tour, and when the four months I had remaining were up, I'd come back and be ready to go to work.

They said, "Absolutely! We totally understand."

So that's what I did. I went straight back to Iraq. It worked out well. The ability to do my job as a physician with the president was contingent on getting a final security clearance anyway. Even if I had started right away, I would have been limited to working in one of the clinics until my clearance was done. I was a little apprehensive about the whole clearance issue. I had heard from others that the clearance process is what prevented them from getting the job. If they deny your clearance, no one ever tells you why. They just say, "Thanks for applying. Good luck with your career, but you can't work here." They do a really in-depth security screening up front during the interview process and give the White House a thumbs up or thumbs down so that they can offer you the job if everything else works out. But the actual clearance usually takes nine to twelve months to complete. I had gotten the thumbs up, but getting a White House badge, getting complete access to the building, and being able to be in the room by yourself with the president was only going to happen after a year of digging in to every aspect of my past. It was one of those things where I was thinking, *Don't get too excited. Don't jinx yourself. You're not there until you're there. Hopefully, everything goes okay with the clearance—knock on wood.* It all worked out, though, and by the time I returned from Iraq and got moved to DC, I was all cleared.

When I first arrived at the White House, the White House Medical Unit was comprised of about twenty-three people. We had six physicians, two army physicians, two navy physicians, and two air force physicians. I was the new junior physician and the only emergency medicine physician. By the time I left, the unit had grown to about sixty-one people. We had ten physicians, sixteen PAs, and eleven or twelve nurses, along with medics, administrators, psychologists, and physical therapists. We had evolved into a really big unit with a much bigger mission.

As soon as I got there, I rapidly moved into a leadership position and took over as the deputy director of the White House Medical Unit in less than three years. By the time I left the White House, I'd had every leadership role possible. I had been the deputy director, the director, the physician to the White House, the appointed physician to the president, assistant to the president, and the appointed chief medical advisor.

As the physician to the president, you have a lot of responsibility but also enjoy a unique level of trust. You're one of the few people, if not one of the only people, in the entire world who can walk up to the president of the United States with a sharp instrument in your hand, and the Secret Service won't stop you. You have the president's life in your hands every single day. Your primary duty is to take care of the president and the First Family, but you have some pretty big collateral responsibilities as well. You are responsible for overseeing the care of everyone involved in serving the president. That includes Air Force One, the presidential helicopter squadron, the White House Communications Agency, the White House Transportation Agency, the Presidential Food Service, Camp David, a large part of the United States Secret Service, and the entire presidential administration and White House staff. You are responsible for the planning and execution necessary to keep everyone safe and healthy, not only while at the White House but while traveling all over the planet. This is the reason the White House Medical Unit is bigger than some might expect.

I was part of the George W. Bush administration for his last three years in office. As the junior physician, I spent the first six months taking care of Vice President Dick Cheney and his family. His primary doctor was Dr. Lew Hofmann, and I was Lew's backup. I did all the trips that Lew didn't want to do, and I spent most nights with the vice president at the Naval Observatory. It was a good duty and a great way to get oriented to the new responsibilities before I moved over to take care of the president and First Family. I traveled with him quite a bit, and the VP was the real deal when it came to making sure you were ready for any medical emergency. He was a very smart and hardworking individual, and I really enjoyed working for him, but as everyone knows from the press, he had some serious cardiac issues. It was a little stressful, but I was very meticulous about packing my medical bag and making sure all the medical contingency plans were checked, double-checked, and triple-checked. A perfect warm-up for taking care of the leader of the free world. He's in much better health now because he's got a new heart, but his heart wasn't in great shape back then. Everybody knew it, and it was open-source, common knowledge that he had suffered several heart attacks. Even President Bush joked with him about it. At the end of the Bush-Cheney term, President Bush had the entire White House Medical Unit over to the Oval Office for a departure photo with him and VP Cheney. Bush was thanking us for doing a great job taking care of him, his family, and his administration. He looked around and looked over at the VP standing next to him and said, "Well, hell, take Dick, for example. When I picked him as VP, I thought for sure he'd be gone by now, but you guys have done a great job keeping him alive." Everyone, including the VP, laughed. President Bush and Vice President Cheney both had a great sense of humor.

I got there in June 2006, and until early 2007, I was predominantly the vice president's doctor. I spent my first Christmas in Jackson Hole, Wyoming, with him. It is a beautiful place to spend the Christmas holiday. For fourteen years, I spent all the holidays with "the family," just not my family. We took lots of precautions to ensure we had everything we needed from the cardiac standpoint, but most of it was just on you as the doctor to make sure you were well trained and ready to do anything and everything you could to save his life if needed. Thank God that day never came. He was a pleasure to take care of, but definitely one of the more complicated patients I had while at the White House.

Once another doctor arrived at the med unit, and I was no longer the junior physician, my time with the vice president was over. I moved over to what we call the POTUS side, taking care of the president and First Family. I worked for Dr. Richard Tubb at that point, who was the appointed physician to the president for George W. Bush. Dr. Tubb was one of my biggest mentors in life and continues to be one of the few people I trust for good advice today. He is the one who made the decision to hire me at the White House. Dr. Tubb put me in charge of taking care of the First Lady and her team. In addition, I served as one of the backup doctors for Dr. Tubb and traveled with President Bush when Dr. Tubb was not with him. The more senior I got, the more I traveled with President Bush.

I traveled anywhere Mrs. Bush went. When she left the White House, I went with her, including when she traveled overseas. I traveled all over the planet with Mrs. Bush and had all kinds of fabulous trips with her. One of the best trips I ever had as a White House physician was one of my very first presidential advances.

As the junior physician, I would travel in advance of the president. My job was to make sure all the equipment and plans were in place and rehearsed before the president, Dr. Tubb, and the rest of the team arrived on Air Force One. I usually went out ten days ahead to ensure we knew where all the hospitals were, what capabilities they had, what equipment we needed to bring, how we were going to get there, whether we needed to bring a surgical team, and a host of other issues.

If the medical capabilities were not adequate, we would bring a military surgical team with us, and it would be my job to make sure they were all set up in the right location and ready to go. We would spend days coordinating all the medical contingency plans with the Secret Service, the presidential helicopter squadron, the White House Communications Agency, Air Force One, and other local and foreign government entities. There was a ton of planning! We always had a well-thought-out contingency plan with multiple backup plans for whatever could happen. You always had to be prepared for the worst-case scenario, such as, what if an IED hits the motorcade, what if the president takes a bullet to the chest, what if the president has a heart attack or stroke, and so on. In addition to all the pre-planning, my job was to take part of the duty with the president when the team arrived. Most of the time, when Dr. Tubb arrived at a location overseas with the president, he would be pretty sleep-deprived and would turn the duty over to me. I would cover the president for the rest of the day or until he was ready to take the duty back.

The first time I was responsible for one of these overseas presidential advances for President Bush was a South and Central American trip. President Bush and Mrs. Bush were doing a swing that included five different countries. Their last stop was my site in Merida, Mexico.

Merida, Mexico, is a beautiful place in the Yucatán Peninsula. I was down there for ten days, and I was checking out all the places the president was going to go. These trips are great because you not only get to see all the cool places he will go, but lots of other exotic locations that the Secret Service deems too dangerous to take him.

I had a great time in Merida preparing the trip. I spent some time on the beautiful beaches and went to some awesome Mayan ruins that are normally off-limits to tourists. But the best part of the trip was to follow. The president and the First Lady arrived in Merida, Mexico, for their last stop on the trip. I was there to receive them as planned. The following day, they woke up, had a couple of quick events, and finished their trip together. President Bush got back on Air Force One and flew to Washington, DC. Mrs. Bush and I got on a Gulfstream jet, along with two Secret Service agents and one of her aides, and flew straight to the Galapagos Islands, where we met Barbara and Jenna. For the next seven or eight days, I was on a cruise boat in the Galapagos Islands with Mrs. Bush, Barbara, and Jenna. It was great. I was working, but I was essentially one of the guests on the boat. I was snorkeling, hiking, and just cruising around the Galapagos on this awesome liveaboard. It was just one of many awesome trips I had with Mrs. Bush. We went all over Africa, Europe, and the Middle East. I even had the opportunity to ride camels through the ancient city of Petra with Mrs. Bush while on a trip in Jordan.

She was a wonderful First Lady, and I loved working for her. We got along well from the very beginning due to the special West Texas attachment we had in common. We both grew up in the same area of Texas. Sometimes when she introduced me, she would say, "Do you know our doctor, Ronny? He's one of us; he's from West Texas." We had that immediate connection. Some of the other doctors also didn't like going to the ranch in Crawford because it was hot, and we worked our butts off there, but it fit right in with the way I was raised, and I loved it. We would spend the entire day working outside, cutting down cedar trees, dragging them into big piles, and burning them. The cedar trees in that part of Texas are like weeds, and they choke out all the other trees. We cleared them out to make room for the oak trees. I was one of the few on the team designated as a chainsaw guy; I had one of the best jobs. It was extremely hard work, and not everyone was excited about it. The rule was, though, if you made the trip to the ranch, you were going to be part of the work party. Everyone was out there. The chief of staff, the staff secretary, the national security advisor, the press secretary, the personal aide, the military aide, the doctor, the nurse, the communications team, and even the Secret Service guys not actively on duty. I soon realized it was about much more than clearing brush. It was an incredible team-building exercise. The team was much stronger as a result of our time together at the ranch.

We also spent a lot of time building bike trails through the woods. President Bush was in phenomenal shape. He was in his sixties, and he used to run a lot before I got to the White House. Apparently, he would go out and run three or four miles and could maintain a 7:30 pace. That's impressive for anybody, and certainly for somebody in their sixties. He was an outstanding athlete.

Now, by the time I got there, his knees had started to wear out a little, and he had started mountain biking. I'm telling you, that guy could get on a mountain bike, and he could kick the butt of somebody twenty years his junior. He was impressive, and he was hard to keep up with. I ran when I was in Iraq, anywhere from six to ten miles a day, and when I came back, I was in great shape, but

I'd never been on a mountain bike before. I eventually started riding with him because it made it easier to keep an eye on him and be there right away if something happened that required medical attention. I would put a small pack on my back with some critical medical equipment and have the nurse and PA who were helping with medical response nearby on an all-terrain vehicle with additional equipment and capabilities.

There were times I'd struggle to keep up with him on the bike, and we'd get to the end, and I would be visibly tired and out of breath. He would immediately call me out and make fun of me. He definitely loved giving me a hard time, but it was all in good fun, and it was his great sense of humor that made working for him enjoyable.

He was a good man; he was never malicious. He treated me like a son; he was very, very good to me. It was a privilege to be on his team and an honor to work for him.

The fact that I stayed on to work for Obama was a real shock to many who knew me and especially those who understood my political leanings.

It was mostly circumstance and, once again, being in the right place at the right time. It turns out that at the end of the Bush administration, all but one of the physicians who were senior to me either retired or moved on to other jobs. They were all very senior to me in rank, and it was time for most of them to leave. Almost overnight, I went from being the most junior in the medical unit to number two in seniority. Although the time on my current orders was up, and it was time for me to leave as well, the Pentagon did not want so much turnover all at once. Dr. Tubb recommended that they keep me there for another three years and move me up to the deputy director job. So, they did.

I was the deputy director of the White House Medical Unit for the first year or so, and then I quickly became the White House Medical Unit director. The physician senior to me was Dr. Jeff Kuhlman. He had been a part of the White House Military Office for a long time. He had worked for Clinton, Bush, and now Obama. Along with Dr. Tubb, he was key in my staying on as the deputy director. He was not only the director at the beginning of the Obama presidency, but he was also the acting physician to the president and, later, the appointed physician to the president for President Obama. Although he and I had our differences at the end of his tenure, he was a mentor to me for many years, and I would not have ended up moving through the ranks in the White House without his support.

Some of the questions I frequently get are: "How did you become the physician to the president?" "Does the president pick his personal physician?" "Is it always a military doctor?" The president definitely picks his physician and decides who is the appointed physician to the president. The way that happens and the timing varies based on the immediate medical needs of the president. Reagan and Bush Senior showed up with their appointed doctor on day one. They were both older and had ongoing medical issues, and as a result, a strong relationship with several civilian physicians before becoming president. Once they arrived at the White House, they offered the appointment to one of the doctors who had already been regularly taking care of them. Clinton, George W. Bush, Obama, and Trump all showed up at the White House in very good physical condition. So appointing a physician to the president was not at the top of their list. They were busy appointing their cabinet and senior staff for the first few months. During that period, it is the senior military physician in the White House Medical Unit who fills the role of the acting physician to the president. Generally, by the time the president gets around to making that decision, they already have a strong relationship and level of trust with one of the military physicians and give the appointment to that individual.

When President Obama arrived at the White House, he was young and healthy. He was focused on setting up his West Wing and cabinet. Dr. Kuhlman, I, and the military members of the White House Medical Unit were already in place on day one and assumed the care for him and his family. He and his entire family were very healthy, so medical was not at the top of their agenda. They got to know the members of the medical unit and were perfectly happy to follow tradition, and after about a year, appoint Dr. Kuhlman, who was a navy captain and director of the White House Medical Unit, as their doctor.

Once he became the physician to the president, he turned over the job of director of the White House Medical Unit to me.

At the end of President Obama's first term, Dr. Kuhlman had decided to retire. He moved on to a civilian job; I immediately became the acting physician to the president, in addition to my duties as director of the White House Medical Unit. Typically, I would have remained in an "acting" role for many months, but because I had been the number two physician for the president and his family for four years, they knew me well and had already developed complete trust and confidence in me and my abilities. I was the acting for less than a week.

I had spent countless hours with the president and First Family by the time Dr. Kuhlman left, and I had a little more of an aggressive and outgoing personality. I was easy to talk to, and it was a good fit for the family. They were very comfortable around me. My clinical skills were excellent, I am a "people person," and I have a great sense of humor.

The staff in the Obama administration were significantly younger than the Bush administration. I spent lots of time with them on trips and got along with everyone very well. When it was time for a change at the beginning of the second term, everyone, including the president, said, "We want Ronny to be the doctor."

So, less than a week in, we were on Air Force One, flying back to DC from an event in Florida. President Obama was walking down the hall, headed towards his office in the front of the plane, and I was walking the opposite way, headed up to the communications deck to talk with the crew about a problem with my internet. As he passed, I turned slightly to let him go by, and he patted me on the shoulder and kept walking. I was headed up the stairs when I heard him say, "Hey, Doc."

I came back down the stairs and said, "Sir?"

He was standing in the middle of the hall with a puzzled look on his face, and he motioned for me to come over. He said, "So, Ronny, let me get this straight, are you, or are you not, my doc now?"

I said, "Well, sir, that is not my call. I don't have anything to do with that decision. That is totally up to you."

He paused and then said, "Okay, consider it done. You're my appointed doc. You're my man."

I said, "Yes, sir!"

He turned and started to walk away. He paused, turned back around, and said, "Hey, doc, do I need to put that in writing or sign something?"

I said, "Yes, sir, that would be great!"

He said, "Okay, tomorrow talk to the chief of staff and let him know it is done and to get the paperwork over to me to sign."

And that was it. I had just been appointed as physician to the president, right there while in-flight on Air Force One. It was completely unexpected, but from that point forward, for the next four years, I was the appointed physician to the president for President Obama.

My entire time at the White House, I never offered my political opinion about anything. That wasn't my job; I was there as an active-duty officer, serving the office of the presidency and the commander in chief. It wasn't my job to have a political opinion; it was my job to make sure the president of the United States was alive and healthy.

Even if you disagree with the person in office, you should still have a certain level of respect for the office itself, which I did. I kept my mouth shut on most issues, but I didn't agree politically with anything that was going on during the Obama administration. As I've said before, I think that the eight years of Obama have led us to where we are today.

That's why we're having issues with race and divisiveness all over our country, because for eight years, everything they did in the Obama administration—I mean everything they did—started and ended with identity politics. Straight versus gay, rich versus poor, black versus white, man versus woman. They made everybody feel like they had to pick a side, and I think that was a strategy. They felt the best way to maintain control was to fracture our society and make everyone believe that everybody else was out to get them. Everybody feels like a victim, and everybody feels like a persecuted group that is being discriminated against by everyone else. We were better united and had a much stronger sense of patriotism throughout the Bush years and probably most of my adult life prior to that.

During the Obama and Trump administrations, my office in the White House was directly below the president's bedroom, so I saw him multiple times throughout the day. I was usually the first one to see him in the mornings and the last one to see him in the evenings. I would also be with him any time he left the White House. If he got into the car, the helicopter, plane, or the elevator, I was there. I was with him at events in DC, throughout the United States, and anywhere in the world that he traveled. The president didn't go anywhere without me.

Because I was with him all the time, I was usually the first to notice when something was not right and if he didn't feel well. If he was walking with a limp, had a cough, or just looked tired, I could tell right away. It was my job to ask the question, "Are you okay? Did something happen? Do you feel sick? Are you sleeping okay?"

Although I made a point not to be involved in the clinical care of the vice president and his family, the doctor and the rest of the team that took care of him worked for me. In addition to my primary duty of taking care of the First Family, I rapidly developed a huge number of patients. Because I traveled everywhere with the entire team, and I was readily available for medical treatment and advice, my patient population exploded during my time with all three presidents. I was eventually taking care of the entire West Wing, East Wing, and everyone who supported them. The First Family, most of the cabinet secretaries, all the assistants to the president, the chief of staff, the national security advisor, the press secretary, the Secret Service, the White House staff, Air Force One, Camp David, the presidential helicopter squadron, the White House Communications Agency, the White House Mess, the military aides, and anyone else who worked in the White House were all my patients.

Over time, I also ended up taking care of many of their immediate and extended family members. I would be on the road traveling with someone, and they would say, "My mother had a stroke," "My sister just delivered a baby and is not doing well," or "My brother-in-law is in California and just got diagnosed with cancer, and we don't know what's going on." I would say, "Give me the doctor's number," and I would call the doctor, find out how bad it was, and then go back and let them know what was happening and reassure them when I could. Occasionally I would discover the patient was getting suboptimal care, and I would have to intervene and get the patient transferred to another hospital. Then I would contact other members of the family and inform them regarding their loved one's condition. None of this was my actual job, but I spent thousands of hours dealing with these issues during my off time at the White House. These people I worked with were my friends, and I wanted to make sure they could do their job and take care of the president and not have to worry about a family member who was sick.

This is one of the reasons I had such a strong relationship with so many people in all three of the past administrations and why they thought so highly of me. Heck, the entire Obama administration used to be fond of me before I retired and got into politics! When you take care of somebody, it's one thing. However, when you take care of their family, particularly their children, people have another level of gratefulness altogether. I was on twenty-four seven, 365 days a year. I'd get phone calls in the middle of the night; I'd get phone calls all weekend. It was a never-ending job.

Over the years at the White House, I had built up a huge medical unit with extensive capabilities. Our mission had grown exponentially, and we worked with counsel in the White House Military

Office to make sure we had all the proper legal authorities. I extended my care to this large group of people because it was in the best interest of the president of the United States. We referred to this as "care by proxy." The idea was that if I took care of the chief of staff or the national security advisor and kept them at their desks at the White House, then I was, by extension, taking care of the president.

These are key people who the president needs to get his job done as commander in chief and head of state. His key people should not be sitting in a waiting room in a hospital somewhere or an emergency room all day, waiting to get evaluated because they have a sore throat or headache.

It was all about convenience and customer service. If someone didn't feel well, I would come to them. I would grab my bag and go to their office. I would check their temperature, blood pressure, and anything else that needed to be done. I could usually treat them right there in their office. I made house calls frequently. I would go to people's homes on my way to or from work, and I would check in on them. I would deliver any medications they needed directly to them and, on occasion, administer IV fluids or IV medications in their home. It was full-blown, over-the-top, concierge executive medicine, and we did it better than anybody else on the planet.

As a result, everyone treated me and my team very well. The entire medical unit had a special place in the hierarchy of the White House. In general, people tend to treat their doctor pretty well, but I had a lot more to offer than any doctor they had ever had before, and they needed me close by.

I never repeated anything I heard. You hear all kinds of crazy stuff in the elevators, on the helicopter, and in the hold rooms. All three of the presidents I have worked for, and their senior staff, always spoke freely around me, as if I weren't there. You really are like a fly on the wall. They know you're in the room, but they don't hold anything back. They say whatever they have to say, and many times, it's a very sensitive conversation taking place, with just you, the president, and one or two other people in the room.

I was never asked to leave the room. I was never aware of any discussions being moved somewhere else because of my presence. I've heard many private and sensitive conservations, and I'll take them all to the grave with me. When someone puts that kind of trust in you, you realize you can never betray that trust.

While I was the director of the White House Medical Unit, I was in charge of all the members of the unit. I always held myself to a high standard, and I ensured that everyone else at the medical unit was doing their job and injected no politics into their duties. I made it clear that would not be tolerated at all. Period. Our mantra and motto were, "The White House Medical Unit, no policy, no politics, just trusted medical care."

A big part of my job was contingency planning and was well suited for my specialty of emergency medicine. But on a day-to-day basis, I was responsible for a lot of family practice-type medicine. It was our job in the White House Medical Unit to address issues like diet, exercise, and avoiding unhealthy habits.

For whatever reason, many people comment to me and tell me they think Obama secretly smoked the whole time he was in the White House. I can tell you definitively, that was not the case. It is public knowledge that he smoked when he got there, but we aggressively worked to help him quit as soon as possible. It was pretty easy because he genuinely wanted to quit. President Obama maintained a healthy lifestyle and paid a lot of attention to his diet and exercise.

He is a smart guy and knew it was important for his long-term health to quit. He, of course, had the urging and support of the First Lady, which always helps. One of the most beneficial things that came from his decision to quit was that many of the staff around him who smoked also quit. If you are around him all day, and he is trying to quit, you don't want to be that person that is smoking around him and making it difficult.

People would ask, how do you know he quit smoking? I would say, because I have an earpiece in my ear all day long, and the Secret Service is calling out every time he moves from one room to the other. I would always hear when he was stepping outside to smoke; you could listen to it called out over the radio. When he stopped smoking, the radio traffic stopped. That was it. I could tell you almost to the day when he quit and didn't smoke anymore.

We worked with the White House chef and the valets who prepared the food for all the presidents, and we made recommendations about eating healthy. Sometimes I'd recommend specific diets they might want to try. They'd also come to me and say, we want to try this diet out for a week. Is it a good idea or a bad idea? I would do the research and figure out the pros and cons. Then I'd work with the people who prepared the food to make it happen if I thought it was a good idea.

Since I got into politics, the Obamas and most of their staff don't have much to do with me anymore, and many of them have let me know how disappointed they are in me. I get it, but they have to understand that I was on active duty, did my job, and did it well, but it doesn't mean that I don't have political opinions just like everyone else. I kept those to myself while on active duty, but I am a member of Congress now, and I represent the most conservative district in the entire country. This is where I grew up, these are my people, and I am going to speak out and represent them!

It is not personal. I disagreed with President Obama and his administration on just about everything they did while he was in office—and still do. However, on a personal level, I enjoyed the family and the staff I got to know during that time.

I had no complaints from President Obama or the Obama family; they loved having me as their physician. The family was good to me, and the president wrote me excellent evaluations. He even promoted me to rear admiral. There were numerous opportunities to let me move on and bring in another physician, but he wanted me to stay and kept me on to the very end. There was never an issue with President Obama or anyone in his administration regarding me or the job I was doing. Quite the opposite, everyone was very pleased with my performance and happy I stayed. It wasn't until I decided to stay on with Trump and became his appointed physician that any issues ever popped up. Once I briefed President Trump's first physical, the daggers came out, and I was a marked man by the liberal media, the Democrats, and many Obama alumni.

5.

Monday night before the 2016 presidential election, I was with President Obama at a Hillary Clinton rally at Independence Hall in Philadelphia, and we were standing backstage. Hillary, Bill, and Chelsea Clinton, Mrs. Obama, Jen Palmieri, and lots of others from the Clinton campaign were also there, along with some big celebrities, such as Bruce Springsteen and Jon Bon Jovi. A big outdoor stage was set up, and a considerable crowd had gathered for the rally and a planned fireworks show at the end. It was a crazy environment I will never forget. I was standing backstage with my medical bag watching it all play out. It was different than countless other rallies I had witnessed. This was a full-blown celebration. A huge victory party! Everybody was high-fiving and hugging, congratulating Hillary and Palmieri for winning. They were even discussing if they should continue with the fireworks or if that would look like they were being presumptuous and rubbing it in. I mean, it was like the election was already over.

I'll admit, I had apparently drunk the Kool-Aid too. Even though I was very depressed and upset that she might be our next president and I was desperately hoping Trump would pull it off and win, I'd been watching MSNBC, CNN, and Fox News, and I thought it was probably over, and she would win it. It didn't matter what you watched; Trump appeared to be down big time, and at this point, there was no way he was going win. At least, that is what the mainstream media and the talking heads had told us. I couldn't believe she was going to be our next president. I just kept thinking, "This sucks!"

I knew I wasn't going to be her doctor. I'd already made plans to leave. I was already a navy rear admiral and had put in over twenty years. I was looking forward to retirement. I thought I'd maybe sit on some boards or do some consulting work, and I was looking forward to moving back to Texas.

I'd told President Obama that I was leaving. I was supposed to accompany him to California on his last flight on Air Force One and then turn my bag over to whoever the incoming administration picked as their doctor. She wasn't elected yet, but I decided that once she was in, I was out. I had no intentions of staying; I was done. It was time for me to move on.

I came to work the following morning. It was Tuesday, and it was Election Day. Everything was normal, and I finished up my work and drove home somewhat late. I was driving home and listening to some of the early exit polls, and there were a few of them coming out, like, "Wow, this looks better for Trump than we thought. Is there something going on here?" Remember, everybody thought Hillary was going to win—everybody. Once I got home, I turned on the TV, and the returns were coming in, and that's when it started getting a little weird.

Trump was doing extremely well! They called Florida, and all these big swing states followed, all coming in for Trump! I remember sitting there at three o'clock in the morning on my couch in my home office, just thinking, *I cannot believe this. He won!* I was freaking out. The press had brainwashed me over the last few months to think that Trump would lose, that the race was already over, so I was shocked when he won. I was also very excited.

The following morning, Wednesday, I went to work after staying up late watching the election results. When I pulled onto West Executive Avenue at the White House to park, there were cars everywhere. Everybody was at work. However, when I walked into the West Wing and made my way over to my office in the White House proper, it was really weird. I felt like I was in a funeral home. People were walking around, and nobody was talking. Some people were even crying. We'd gone from Monday night, where it was a full-blown victory celebration, to Wednesday morning, where it was like somebody had died. For days after that, people were solemn.

On President Obama's last night in the White House, he invited a handful of people—and I mean only twelve to fifteen of us—upstairs to his residence to sit out on the Truman Balcony and have drinks. It was just me, Valerie Jarrett, Susan Rice, Ben Rhodes, Marvin Nicholson, Pete Souza, and the rest of his inner circle. Everybody was reminiscing. It had been eight whole years, and we couldn't believe it was over.

He told everybody to roam about and do whatever we wanted. We had free rein of the residence, so people were walking around the Lincoln Bedroom and the Queens' Bedroom and in the area where his private office was. It was a nice night; you could see the South Grounds Fountain, the Washington Monument, and the Jefferson

Memorial from the balcony. He was basically saying to all of us, "Hey, it's been a great ride, and I want to tell everybody thank you." It was thoughtful and a very gracious gesture.

They never assumed I was a liberal. They knew I was conservative; they knew that I probably disagreed with them politically, but they never imagined I'd be going into politics. I mean, no one, including myself, saw that coming. They didn't have any misconceptions about where I fit politically; I think they knew that I was on the right and they were on the left, but I was their doctor, and they trusted me. I'd never betrayed their trust in eight years, and to this day, I would never betray that trust, period. I had taken great care of them; I took care of their families and their extended families, so I believe they overlooked that my beliefs were on the other side of the aisle.

I think about the friends I had in that administration who don't have much to do with me now because I'm so outspoken on the right. I traveled the world with these people. I got to know them and their families. People like Marvin Nicholson, who was the president's trip director and personal aide—I love that guy. To this day, I'd do anything for him. Reggie Love, who was his personal aide—I love Reggie, and we got along great. Alyssa Mastromonaco, the president's deputy chief of staff—loved her. Pete Souza, the president's photographer, doesn't care for me these days, but I liked Pete.

All of these people were good friends of mine, and so I kind of regret that I've lost many of them in the process. But you do what you got to do. You must make choices in life, and I decided that I would step up to the plate and be a loud voice aimed at protecting the future of my kids and our country. In doing so, I had to sacrifice a few friendships, and that's just the way it is.

I don't think that they saw me as a potential politician. I didn't see myself that way, so I never talked about it; I never showed any interest in it. Even after I left the Obama administration, I never showed any interest in it until the last year of the Trump administration.

I got a few letters from some people, a few emails or texts from people telling me they were super disappointed that I'd decided to go down this path. I would tell them, "I still consider you a friend, and I'm sorry you feel that way. It is what it is. You should understand; if anybody should understand, you should. I'm in politics now, and I'm a Republican in the most Republican district in the country. People who worked in the White House should get that."

As I mentioned earlier, I was initially going to leave the White House with Obama and retire. I was already preparing for the transition and would go over to the Walter Reed National Military Medical Center and close out for a couple of months, get all my retirement paperwork submitted, and then be gone. That was my plan.

What happened is, after Trump won the election, his team had to set up a transition plan. Most of the people working for Trump at the time hadn't worked in the White House before, and they didn't know anything about transitioning into the West Wing and setting up a presidential administration. So they did what every administration does and reached out to the people who had most recently been there. Turns out these were all Bush people, and they all knew me well. I had worked with most of them in the Bush administration, and I had taken care of them and their families. They loved me, and as soon as they found out I was still at the White House, they called me up. It was just weeks before the presidential inauguration when they first engaged me. I was on Christmas vacation with the Obama family in Hawaii. They called me up, and they said, "We need you to hang around; we want you to stay." I said, "I'm not staying; there's no way."

They just kept coming after me. I insisted I wasn't staying; I explained that I already had plans to get out of the military and retire. I'd already found a doctor who was currently in the White House Medical Unit and supposed to take over for me and be President Trump's new physician. He had been in New York with the Trump team for a couple of months and was supposed to be developing a relationship with President-elect Trump. That way, on Inauguration Day, we could switch out, and I could leave.

He was an excellent physician but was a little bit more of an introvert than I am, and President Trump and most of his team are pretty outgoing. The chemistry wasn't right, so they said, "This isn't working out and we want you to stay." They continued to pursue me.

I came back from Christmas vacation, and it was about a week before the inauguration. They said, "You have absolutely, positively got to stay." I still refused.

Well, Joe Hagin, the deputy chief of staff in the Bush administration, was overseeing most of the transition and was coming back to be part of the Trump administration. Joe would be the new deputy chief of staff for Trump. I knew Joe well, and he brought on a guy named Dan Walsh and put him in charge of the transition team. Dan had been the Coast Guard military aide for President Bush. We worked closely in the Bush administration and had become good friends. Dan was also planning to join the Trump team and ultimately ended up being the director of the White House Military Office and later the deputy chief of staff for President Trump.

These two guys persisted and were the reason I stayed. Especially Dan. I trusted him, and I knew he would make sure my career didn't suffer if I stayed. The decision was Joe's, so I told him I wanted to sit down and discuss it. I had already decided I was going to stay, but I thought I would use this as an opportunity to start off on the right foot in the new Trump administration. I said, "Here's the deal. If I stay, this is what I need. I'm going to be the appointed physician to the president in writing on day one. I want to be a deputy assistant to the president on day one; I'm going to be considered senior staff. I'm going to maintain my autonomy and independence from the White House Military Office. I will work directly for the chief of staff on day-to-day issues, and directly for the president on anything and everything involving medical care for him and the First Family."

I was expecting a little bit of a negotiation, but they were like, "Done, done, done, done, done…. You got it." They initially wanted me to stay for the complete term, and I said, "I'm not going to do that; there's no way." They said, "Well, we need you to stay for a couple of years," and I said, "I'll stay for six to twelve months, and I'll find you somebody who can take my place that you're comfortable with; I'll make sure that there's a good turnover, and then I'm out of here." They said, "Okay, fair enough." I had no idea that I would get so tight with President Trump and want to stay long term, but that is exactly what happened.

The first time I met him was when he came to the White House right after being elected. President and Mrs. Obama invited him and Mrs. Trump up to the White House as is traditionally done. Mrs. Obama immediately took Mrs. Trump upstairs to have tea and show her the residence.

President Obama walked President Trump from the South Lawn through the Diplomatic Reception Room and straight into my office. President Obama said, "I want to introduce you to Ronny. He's my doctor. Ronny's a navy admiral. He takes excellent care of me, and he runs a whole team here that takes care of my family and all the staff. Ronny will not be here when you get here. He's leaving with me, but he'll have another doctor who will be your doctor when you get here."

Trump said, "How are you doing? Nice to meet you." I shook his hand, and they walked out. That was immediately after the election, so I had no idea I would be staying at that point. It wasn't until the day before the inauguration that I decided I was committed to staying.

I said, "I'm going to do this," and put my retirement on the back burner. I knew the next thing I had to do was speak to President Obama because I was supposed to be going to Palm Springs with him after the inauguration for his last flight on Air Force One. I talked to President Obama the morning of the inauguration and said, "Sir, I need to speak to you about something."

"What is it?" he asked.

"I'm not going to be flying to California with you today."

"What do you mean? What's wrong?"

I said, "Well, you're not going to like this, but I'm staying around.... I'm going to stay and make the transition with the Trump team."

"What?" he asked, shocked.

"They're in a bind, and I owe it to the office." I then explained it to him, the same way they had explained it to me, "Ronny, we have all kinds of unknowns right now while trying to set up the entire White House, we have all these balls in the air, and the Medical Unit is hitting on all cylinders. You're doing a great job, and we need you to stay and take this off our plate."

I explained that to President Obama and said, "Sir, I feel like I have to do this; I know it's not what you wanted. It wasn't what I was planning on doing, but I feel like I need to stay and help them make the transition and lighten their load."

He wasn't happy with it. He said, "I'm not comfortable with it, Ronny; I don't like it," and then he stressed to me, "If you do this, you need to leave as soon as you can. You don't need to hang around; you need to get in and out."

I said, "All right, I'll get out as fast as I can." Obama disapproved, but he wasn't nasty about it; he just let me know he didn't like it.

That was a strange day. I got in the motorcade and left the White House with President Obama that morning and headed to the Capitol. I followed President Obama into the Capitol and to the stage. I stood just inside the door leading out onto the inauguration stage on the West side of the US Capitol when he and President Trump turned over at 12:01 on January 20. I passed the bag I was carrying that was designed specifically for President Obama across the hall to the doctor who was covering President-elect Trump, and he passed the bag he was carrying that was designed specifically for President Trump to me. Obama walked out, and he followed Obama, and Trump walked out, and I followed Trump. I had a quick opportunity to tell Obama good-bye, and he got on the helicopter, flew to Andrews Air Force Base, got on the plane, and then left for Palm Springs. He didn't know I would stay long term, and he certainly didn't know I would be running for office one day, but neither did I. When President Trump was done at the Capitol, I got back in the motorcade with him and went back to the White House. We pulled up on the South Lawn of the White House and walked into the Diplomatic Reception Room. Eric, Laura, Don Jr., Vanessa, Ivanka, and Jared were there, along with all of the president's grandkids. All five of Don's kids and all three of Ivanka's kids were running around climbing on the furniture. I had just left the White House with President Obama, Mrs. Obama, Sasha, and Malia, and Sasha and Malia were both essentially grown-up at that point; they weren't kids anymore. Suddenly, I realized, *Wow, I better brush up on my pediatric medicine; I have all these little kids to take care of now too!*

It was great; they were fun. I was pleasantly surprised at how hospitable the entire Trump family turned out to be. They all introduced themselves, and I was shocked at how nice, down-to-earth, and approachable they were.

I also realized how disoriented many of the staff and family must be, many having never spent any real time in the White House. Reince Priebus was the brand-new chief of staff, and he walked up to me and said, "Do you know where the Oval Office is?"

I said, "Yes, sir, I know where it is."

"Can you take me there?"

"Yes, sir, I can take you there."

We left the Diplomatic Reception Room, and I took him to the Oval Office. When we were there, he said, "Do you know where the Martin Luther King Jr. bust is?"

"Yes, sir, it's right behind you, next to the door."

He turned around and said, "That's what I thought." Then he took a picture of it and said, "People are already posting that President Trump took the Martin Luther King Jr. bust out of the Oval Office. What a bunch of assholes." I couldn't have agreed more. Turns out that was just the beginning of the mainstream media's relentless attempts to lie and mischaracterize President Trump.

Some people who didn't know me didn't know how I got there. A few mid-level people said, "Weren't you with Obama too?" They were confused about it, but I explained why. I didn't stress the fact that I had been President Obama's appointed physician. I just said, "I'm a navy physician, and I'm here on orders."

There were many other people in my same situation. The five military aides from the five branches had also made the transition. In addition, people in the White House Communications Agency, Air Force One, the helicopter squadron, and all members of the White House Military Office who were active duty had stayed. In most people's minds, I was just grouped in with these folks.

They said, "You know he's on active duty, so that's why he's still here." The people who knew that I was Obama's appointed physician were never suspicious of me because they were very close to Joe Hagin and Dan Walsh, who had brought me on board, and many other people who had known me in the Bush years. They immediately thought, *He's one of us.* Everybody either knew and trusted me or trusted those that knew me. It all worked out for me, and I was readily accepted by all. There were many Bush alumni that ended up in the Trump administration, including Shealah Craighead. Shealah was Mrs. Bush's photographer and was now going to be President Trump's official photographer. She and I had already traveled all over the world together with Mrs. Bush and were great friends. There were many other old friends joining the team, and it made me feel much better about my decision to stay. It was like we were getting much of the old gang back together again.

It did not take me long to get to know President Trump. I had a unique situation that allowed me to spend a lot of time with him early on. My office in the White House is located directly below the president's bedroom and directly across from the elevator he comes down every morning. I was usually the first person he saw in the mornings and the last person he saw in the evenings. He was routinely awake hours before anyone else showed up for work in the West Wing. He would be watching the morning news, tweeting, reading the paper, and talking on the phone before heading down. By the time he hit the bottom of that elevator, he was looking for someone to talk to. I was often there, and he would engage me on the issues of the day. We would start talking, and he would say, "Walk with me," so I would. We would walk down the West Colonnade, the Oval Colonnade, and into the back of the Oval Office. His chief of staff, national security advisor, CIA briefer, or others would be in the outer Oval Office waiting for him. I would finish up my conversation with him, walk out, they would walk in, and his day would begin. I made it a habit to walk him to work on a regular basis. This is what allowed him to quickly develop a high level of trust and confidence in me and what allowed me to develop genuine respect and admiration for him. He was a straightforward, ordinary guy who was easy to talk to.

Many people had trouble getting on the president's schedule and finding time to see him. Everybody wants face time with the president, and they are always competing for a place on his schedule. That wasn't the case for me. Given the proximity of my office and my job as his personal physician, I had as much time with him as I needed. Because of the relationship I had with him as his physician, nobody questioned what I was talking to him about, what my agenda was, or if it was important enough for me to speak to him. If I said I needed to talk to him, I'd talk to him. It was that simple.

The chief of staff is obviously a very key role in the White House. They are all different. Like all presidents, President Trump had several. His first was Reince Priebus. Everyone really liked Reince, and so did I. They all have their strengths and weaknesses, and Reince's weakness was that he wasn't a great gatekeeper. In his defense, he probably didn't think that was his primary job, and maybe it wasn't, but the president's schedule was not well protected. People regularly just dropped in the Oval Office to talk to the president, and in my opinion, this was disadvantageous to him. When General John Kelly took over as chief of staff later in the year, the pendulum swung to the other extreme. He locked the process down, almost to a point where it was detrimental because nobody could talk to the president unless they ran it by him. And that's not always great either.

But as I said, I was the exception to that. I never ran anything past General Kelly. I would talk to the president before General Kelly even saw the president in the morning. General Kelly supported my relationship with the president and never had an issue with me being an exception to the rule. Nobody ever questions the doctor about their agenda. Most people in the White House are scared to inject themselves into the private medical issues of the First Family. It is a good policy to have because the three families I worked for didn't want staff members trying to make that any of their business. That really works to your advantage as the doctor because no one ever asks you what you were talking to the president about.

I'd talked to Obama about non-medical stuff all the time too. I spent eight years with him, so I obviously got to know him very well during that time. I wasn't walking Obama to work every morning. However, I did occasionally. So when Trump got there, I knew what I was doing. During my time with President Bush and my first three years at the White House, my office was not in the White House. I was located in the White House Medical Unit office space in the Old Executive Office Building right next to the West Wing. I did, however, develop a similar bond with President Bush because we had a tight West Texas connection. I was comfortable around all three of the presidents, and I felt like I could talk to any of them about anything, whether it was a medical-related issue or not. I will say that Trump was the easiest to engage in conversation and definitely the most fun to talk to.

During my time with President Obama, I tried to keep politics out of our conversations. During my time with President Trump, I could speak freely. Trump knew where I stood on everything, and it was almost always the same place he was. I shared a lot of my political opinions with Trump because he and I were politically aligned.

I had watched him on the campaign trail, so I was confident when he first arrived at the White House that we saw things through the same lens. One day, I got on the helicopter, and he'd been meeting with some flag and general officers from the Pentagon. They were talking about transgender issues in the military. President Trump wanted to overturn the Obama policy that allowed transgender people to join the military. He was totally against it, but many of the flag and general officers in the military were caving to the woke and culturally destructive garbage that's taking over our country right now.

This had been a DoD policy during the Obama administration. They were starting to let transgender people serve in the military, and it wasn't just if you were already in the military and wanted to be transgender. They were actively encouraging transgender people to enlist in the military.

Now there was a new sheriff in town, and President Trump made it pretty clear he did not think this was in the best interest of the military or our national security. He wanted to change it, but the generals didn't want him to. They said, "Sir, it's not the right time right now because politically, it's going to blow up." Apparently, the consensus among the generals and some of the political advisors from the West

Wing also in attendance was, "You can do this, sir, but you need to give it a little more time.... What we need to do is roll it out over time. We need to commission a study for the next six months and study the impact of transgender people in the military, and then when we get the study back, we can readdress this and change the policy." They told him they could reverse the policy, but it would take a year or so. They were trying desperately to get him off the idea of immediately changing the Obama policy.

He reluctantly told them to go ahead with their plan, but he wasn't happy. He got on the helicopter with me; I was sitting across from him, and he said, "Doc, what do you think about transgender people in the military?"

I paused for a second and then said, "You want to know what I think off the record?"

"Yes, off the record, tell me what you think."

And I said, "I think it's bullshit, sir.

"First off, it's a big issue with morale and good order and discipline; the military is not a social experiment. We have people coming into the military because they want to go through the transition process. They want to spend taxpayer dollars on hormonal replacement therapy, transition surgeries and all this other crap. They're not deployable; they can't deploy anywhere during this period, and all this takes a year and a half to two years. So, for two years, all they're doing is sucking up taxpayer dollars. They're not actually in a deployable state. If my wife wants breast surgery, she can't get it because it's an elective procedure. But if I want breast surgery because I'm, quote, transgender, they'll do it and call it clinically indicated. That's ridiculous; it's an elective procedure either way. The taxpayers don't want to pay for this, and it's not the right thing for the military or our national security."

Trump agreed, and he said, "We're getting rid of this policy." He got off the helicopter, walked past the press, and boarded Air Force One. Immediately the next morning he sent out a tweet announcing that after consultation with his generals and military experts, we would no longer allow transgenders in the military. The press went crazy!

Everybody in the Pentagon was flipping out. Who was the military advisor that he was talking to? The Pentagon sent out an email to the flag officers in the navy, demanding to know who had spoken to the president about the transgender subject. I just kept my mouth shut; I didn't say anything, but it was me...it was me on the helicopter.

As far as the press was concerned, Obama was still the messiah. They worshipped the ground he walked on. So without any knowledge about his medical condition whatsoever, all of them would have reported, "He is the healthiest, sexiest, best president we've ever had." That's just how they were. I distinctly remember when President Obama first got to the White House. He would walk outside near the press corps, and they would see him and start fawning all over him to the point where they were almost incapacitated. They loved the guy.

It was a different story when Trump showed up. He'd walk out, and they just wanted to spit on him. If Obama was the messiah, then Trump was the Antichrist as far as the press was concerned. When I did Obama's physical, there wasn't any demand to brief it in person. I'd put together a written brief that I would give to the press secretary regarding the president's physical exam, and I would provide all the objective data. I would say, "This is what his blood pressure is, his pulse...these are the medications he's on." I'd lay it all out, and the White House would give it to the press, and the press would go,

"Okay, great, just like we thought; the guy is super healthy." That was the extent of it, and nobody ever pushed back on it. Nobody ever tried to question my methods, my honesty, or ask any hard or probing questions. I did three physicals on Obama in my four years as his appointed physician, so I did one about every other year because he was healthy; he didn't need to have one every year.

When Trump got in office, there were immediately all kinds of questions about his mental capacity and physical fitness to do the job. Nothing was driving that; he didn't do anything, say anything; they were looking for any reason to get rid of the guy because they could not believe he was president. They were trying before Trump even got into office to get rid of him, and this was just one of many ways that they were trying to do it.

They thought, *We're going to give this one a shot too. We're going to say he's not mentally and physically qualified to be president. Oh my God, he eats McDonald's and Kentucky Fried Chicken all the time; he's overweight, he must be a ticking time bomb just waiting to die.... He has to be the unhealthiest president we've ever had.* The narrative from the press and social media was disgusting, factually inaccurate, and completely dishonest.

Just before he arrived at the White House, he had a physical by a doctor in New York, Dr. Bornstein, who turned out to be a quack. You do a physical once every one to two years for most people, so I didn't do it right away. I did, however, gather up all his medical records for the past twenty years and put together a plan for a complete and thorough physical that I planned to do about a year into his presidency. I was pleasantly surprised that he was very healthy for his age, didn't have any ongoing medical issues that needed to be addressed, and was only on a few routine medications. He seemed to be doing great, and I felt like we had time to plan the physical and do it according to my anticipated timeline. About a year into his presidency, I said, "Sir, we're a year out; we probably should do a physical exam, just an annual physical. The press will be asking about it…. They've already been talking a lot about it over the past few weeks. We should get ahead of this and do the annual physical."

He said, "Okay, let's get it scheduled." And we got it done. I took him up to Walter Reed; I conducted a thorough, thorough physical. I mean, I had thirteen specialists see him. I didn't do this physical by myself; I was assisted by an entire committee of top-of-the-line specialty doctors at Walter Reed, including ones who specialized in dermatology, orthopedics, gastroenterology, ophthalmology, urology, pulmonary medicine, otolaryngology, and cardiology. The cardiologist did his heart exam. The pulmonologist did his lung exam and pulmonary function testing, the dermatologist did his skin exam, and so on.

He got a very, very thorough physical exam. I told him he could do a better job with his diet, and he would be a little healthier if he exercised and lost some weight, but other than that, he was in outstanding shape for his age. He really was in excellent physical condition for his age. He has never smoked, never drank in his entire life, and it's made a difference. I put him on the treadmill for an exercise stress test followed by an echocardiogram; he crushed the treadmill. I was truly astonished at how well he did. He was in the top 10 percent for endurance in his age group. His performance on the treadmill was great, and the follow-on echocardiogram showed his heart muscle was functioning very well. It was very, very good; it even surprised me. We walked away from his physical, and I was looking at all the objective data, and I was like, *Damn, this guy smoked his physical. He's much fitter than I even thought he was.* We did CT scans of his coronary arteries, and he had a little bit of calcium, but it was low for his age. His cholesterol was low, his heart rate was normal, his blood pressure was normal, his fasting blood sugar was normal; he didn't have high blood pressure, he didn't have diabetes, he didn't have any medical problems we could find. In addition to the thorough physical exam that most presidents periodically receive, I also did something that had never been done. I did a cognitive screening exam. I did this for one reason and one reason only, because the mainstream media had been relentless in suggesting that the president had a cognitive issue. I was around him every day, and I knew without a doubt that he did not. He was sharp as a tack, and his memory was better than most, including mine. He hadn't done anything while president to give the press or anyone else the impression that he had any cognitive issues. They just didn't like him and didn't like his style. They hated him and would propagate anything they had in order to try and get rid of him, even if it meant that they had to create the false narrative that he had cognitive issues. I approached the president with this proposal. I said, "If you want to address these cognitive accusations, now is the time to do it when we do your physical exam."

He said, "What does that entail?"

I explained it to him, and he said, "Sounds good to me. What is the downside?"

I said, "Well, we will have to let the press know we did it and give them the results even if they're not good."

He said, "Let's do it!"

So, I spoke to multiple psychologists and psychiatrists around the country and asked them what the best cognitive screening exam would be to do as part of a routine physical exam for a person in the president's age group. The universal answer was the MoCA (Montreal Cognitive Assessment). This is a cognitive screening exam designed to detect early mental decline associated with things like stroke, Alzheimer's, age-related dementia, Parkinson's disease, and other cognitive diseases.

We administered the test to the president as part of his annual exam, and as I expected, he passed it without any difficulty whatsoever. In fact, he scored thirty out of thirty, a perfect score.

After reviewing all the results with the other physicians who assisted in the exam, I was ready to move forward with the published report. I was pleasantly surprised that there was essentially nothing to explain, and I thought this would be easy for me to brief. I was going to write it up like I normally did and give it to him and then pass it on to the press secretary for release. But the president said, "I think you need to talk to the press; I want you to go out there, and I want you to brief it to them and answer all the questions they have."

I said, "Okay. Is there anything you don't want me to talk about?"

He said, "I don't care, I don't have anything to hide. You can talk about any damn thing you want."

On the day of the press briefing, I walked straight from my office to the press secretary's office to meet up with Sarah Huckabee Sanders. I didn't prepare at all for this briefing. Nothing—I mean zero. We were about to go out there and do it, and Sarah said, "Doctor, we'll go out there, I'll introduce you, you'll go up to the podium, go over his physical, maybe answer a couple of questions.... You should be no more than ten to fifteen minutes, max."

I said, "Okay."

Sarah and I stopped by the Oval Office before going out to the press briefing room to let the president know I was about to brief the physical. Sarah told the president it would probably only take me about fifteen minutes. As I was walking out of the Oval, the president said, "Ronny, you stay up there, and you answer every damn question they ask you. You stay up there, and as long as they ask questions, you answer the questions."

I said, "Yes, sir."

I was up there for an hour and ten minutes! It was insane. They were asking me all kinds of stupid questions. They ran out of stuff to ask me; they started asking me questions that were so stupid and ridiculous that I couldn't believe it. It got so bad that the rest of the press all over the country began criticizing the White House press pool, saying that they embarrassed themselves with the silly questions they asked.

They had Sanjay Gupta and all these medical correspondents from CNN and MSNBC in there. The room was packed; it was utterly full; there were more people in there than I've ever seen. The medical correspondents who were in there were not normally in the press briefing room. They were basically there as political assassins to cut my head off and make the president look bad; that's why they were there.

They came at me with everything they had. All I did was get up there and give them the facts; I was super objective; I didn't get emotional about anything; I went over the physical. Every time they asked me a question, I answered it, and I elaborated on it. They didn't have a leg to stand on. They got frustrated, and that's when they started asking foolish questions.

When it was over, it worked out well: the president was excited about it because, in the days to follow, all of the questions about him being cognitively and physically unfit to be president just went away;

they were gone. My brief just took it off the table completely. The president was happy to put that to bed and get on with his job. He also liked that the press looked foolish in the process, which was a feather in my cap.

When it was over, a couple of people said, "You're going to be on *Saturday Night Live* with that one." I was like, "I'm not going to be on *Saturday Night Live*; that's ridiculous." I honestly didn't think I would be, but I told my wife, "Everybody's saying they think I'm going to be on *Saturday Night Live*. Should we watch?" We turned it on, and lo and behold, it was the cold open of the show. I thought, *Wow! How crazy is this?*

The whole process of doing the annual physical exam went well, but I tell people all the time I was naïve about what really happened that day. I was an active-duty navy admiral just doing my assigned job at the White House. What I didn't realize at first was that that was the day I got the Trump stamp on me. That was the day I became public enemy number one for the Far Left and the liberal press, and they decided that day that if they ever had a chance to cut my heart out, they were going to take it. I didn't realize that until months later, but looking back, after all the drama surrounding my nomination for secretary of veterans affairs, I realized that was the day they learned to hate me. That was the day I went from being the navy doctor who took care of Bush, Obama, and Trump to being just Trump's doctor. And that is fine with me!

In Outer Oval Office briefing President Obama
Photo by White House Photographer Pete Souza

Humanitarian trip to Africa with former president Bush in June 2013, renovating a medical clinic in Zambia
Photo by Bush Center Photographer Laura Crawford

Christmas 2017 at the White House with President and Mrs. Trump
Photo by White House Photographer Allaina Parton

Family at Camp David during the Bush administration

Ronny in Medical Cabin of Air Force One on the way to President Bush's ranch in Texas

nny in Iraq in October 2005

ADMIRAL
YOU ARE THE GREATEST! AndDonald

mily in Oval Office with President Trump in April 2018
oto by White House Photographer Shealah Craighead

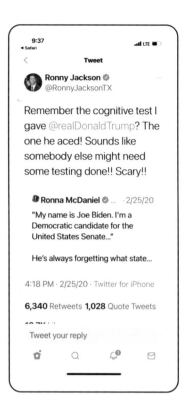

Ronny in medical tent of Shock Trauma Plato while serving in Iraq in 2006

Tweet that inspired President Obama's email of disapproval

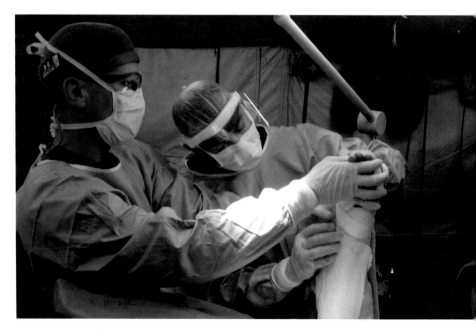

Ronny with orthopedic surgeon Mike Kazel after operating on a wounded Marine in Ir

Ronny and President Bush working on a chainsaw at Texas ranch

Ronny and family, Christmas 2019

Ronny and parents at victory party after winning runoff election in July 2020

Jane's truck on the campaign trail in Shamrock, Texas, during the 2020 congressional campaign

Photo by Jane Jackson

1. Name (Last, First MI Suffix)	2. Grade	3. Desig	4. SSN			
Jackson, Ronny L	RDML	2700	▮▮▮			

POTENTIAL TRAITS	NOB	Very Low (1)	Low (2)	Avg (3)	High (4)	Very High (5)
40. Fiscal Planning/Organizational Skills	☐	☐	☐	☐	☒	☐
41. Personal Growth	☐	☐	☐	☐	☒	☐
42. Professional Growth	☐	☐	☐	☐	☐	☒
43. Potential Leading Change	☐	☐	☐	☐	☐	☒
44. Strategic Thinking	☐	☐	☐	☐	☐	☒

45. Performance Trait Average	Individual 4.66		Reporting Senior 4.66	

46. Future Assignments: I recommend the following assignments for this individual (three)

MEDICAL OFFICER OF THE MARINE CORPS	JOINT STAFF SURGEON	EXECUTIVE MEDICINE

47. Comments

An exceptional physician and leader, Ronny has been a dedicated and valuable member of my team. He has tirelessly ensured not only my health and well being, but that of my family and entire administration. He has earned my complete trust and respect. Continue to groom and promote this highly capable officer.

48. Signature Of Reporting Senior

49. Signature of Individual Evaluated. "I have seen this report, been apprised of my performance, and understand my right to make a statement.

☐ I intend to submit a statement   ☒ I do not intend to submit a statment

50. Typed name, grade, command, UIC and signature of Regular Reporting Senior on Concurrent Report

Annual Officer Fitness Report by President Obama for Rear Admiral Ronny Jackson

Document scan by Ronny Jackson

Ronny walking with President Obama and team back to Marine One after visit to Walter Reed National Military Medical Center

Photo by White House Photographer Pete Souza

President Obama presenting Dr. Jackson with birthday cake on Air Force One as he turns forty-four years old

Photo by White House Photographer Pete Souza

President Obama and Ronny's son putting the rank of rear admiral on Ronny's uniform during the Oval Office promotion ceremony

Photo by White House Photographer Pete Souza

The Jackson family with President Obama after the promotion ceremony in the Oval Office
Photo by White House Photographer Pete Souza

The Jackson family during first Christmas at the White House with President and Mrs. Bush
Photo by White House Photographer Kim Hewitt

Ronny boarding Marine One on South Lawn of White House
Photo by White House Photographer Andrea Hanks

Dr. Jackson with President Trump before boarding Marine One after his first annual physical exam
Photo by White House Photographer Shealah Craighead

Dr. Jackson in the White House Press Briefing Room while briefing the press regarding the results of President Trump's first annual physical exam
Photo by White House Photographer Andrea Hanks

Ronny, President Trump, and senior staff in the Oval Office just before the announcement of Rear Admiral Jackson as nominee for Secretary of Veterans Affairs
Photo by White House Photographer Shealah Craighead

Ronny and family with President Trump during drop-by visit in Oval Office
Photo by White House Photographer Shealah Craighead

Ronny and President Trump in the president's office aboard Air Force One
Photo by White House Photographer Shealah Craighead

Ronny and President Trump greeting Governor Greg Abbott after descending the steps of Air Force One in Texas
Photo by White House Photographer Shealah Craighead

Ronny boards Marine One on the South Lawn of the White House with fellow senior staff from the Trump administration
Photo by White House Photographer Andrea Hanks

FITNESS REPORT & COUNSELING RECORD (07/08) (cont'd)

RCS BUPERS 1610-1

1. Name (Last, First MI Suffix)				2. Grade	3. Desig	4. SSN		
Jackson, Ronny L				RDML	2700	███████		

POTENTIAL TRAITS	NOB	Very Low (1)	Low (2)	Avg (3)	High (4)	Very High (5)
40. Fiscal Planning/Organizational Skills	☐	☐	☐	☐	☐	☒
41. Personal Growth	☐	☐	☐	☐	☐	☒
42. Professional Growth	☐	☐	☐	☐	☐	☒
43. Potential Leading Change	☐	☐	☐	☐	☐	☒
44. Strategic Thinking	☐	☐	☐	☐	☐	☒

45. Performance Trait Average	Individual 5.00	Reporting Senior 5.00

46. Future Assignments: I recommend the following assignments for this individual (three)

MEDICAL OFFICER OF THE MARINE CORPS	JOINT STAFF SURGEON	EXECUTIVE MEDICINE

47. Comments

Dr Jackson is a great Doctor + Leader - "2 STAR MATERIAL"

48. Signature Of Reporting Senior	49. Signature of Individual Evaluated. "I have seen this report, been apprised of my performance, and understand my right to make a statement. ☐ I intend to submit a statement ☒ I do not intend to submit a statment
50. Typed name, grade, command, UIC and signature of Regular Reporting Senior on Concurrent Report	

Annual Officer Fitness Report by President Trump for Rear Admiral Ronny Jackson

Document scan by Ronny Jackson

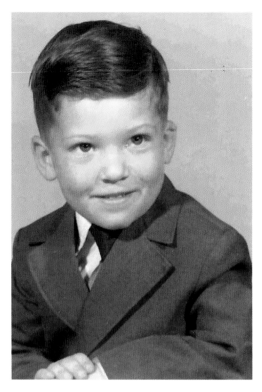

Ronny, age four
Photo courtesy of Norma Jackson

Ronny at age seven with parents, Waymon and Norma, and his brother and sister, Gary and Stacy
Photo courtesy of Norma Jackson

Ronny and Jane on their wedding day in 1993

Ronny with his children, Libby, Ben, and Matt, in 2002
Photo courtesy of Jane Jackson

6.

I had never really thought about being a cabinet secretary. It's not something that ever crossed my mind. I had no idea that President Trump or anyone in the administration had ever considered me in that regard. However, I think there were a couple of discussions that I wasn't privy to early on. Here's what I do know:

Everybody in the administration knew for months and months before President Trump nominated me for the secretary of veterans affairs that David Shulkin was on his way out. I knew it, David knew it, and most people at the White House and the VA knew it. David was a friend of mine, and he and I had even talked about it.

I think there had been some bumps in the road with David and some senior officials in the administration, and some key people wanted him gone. The president may have occasionally gotten frustrated with David, but that happens with all cabinet secretaries and the president at times. Overall, the president liked David, but some of the other people in the administration encouraged the president to eliminate Shulkin and replace him with somebody else. The president had already decided it was time for a change, but these people were aggressively advocating for sooner than later. The main issue at the time seemed to revolve around the upcoming new electronic health record in the Department of Veterans Affairs. David Shulkin had been the secretary during the Obama administration and was the only cabinet secretary who President Trump decided to keep. I knew David from the Obama days, and he and I got along well. Apparently, many people in the Trump administration felt he had outlived his usefulness.

I spoke to the president a couple of times about it. "What do you think about Shulkin?" he asked me. "Do you think he's doing a good job?"

I always defended David, so I said, "I think he's doing a good job, sir."

Looking back, I realize that there were people who just wanted him out because they wanted their guy in there, and unfortunately, that's too often how it works in government. My point was everybody knew that David was probably going to be leaving sometime very shortly; it wasn't a matter of if but a matter of when. I realized later there was a cadre of people in the White House, in the Department of Defense, the Department of Veterans Affairs, and in the Senate, who felt it was their duty to the country to pick the president's cabinet for him. General Kelly was one of them.

He was the chief of staff at the time, and I'd always liked General Kelly and felt that he had my best interests at heart. I don't feel that way now, but I did at the time. I know that there were conversations about who would replace David Shulkin, and these people saw that as an opportunity to influence the process. I don't necessarily think there's anything wrong with that. Suppose you're the president's chief of staff or a committee chair on the Veterans' Affairs Committee in the Senate, overseeing the confirmation hearings. In that case, it's not necessarily bad that you're thinking, *If he's going to be leaving shortly, who would we like to see in that position, and how can we start working the process so they're considered for the job?*

It turns out that the president had also spent some time thinking about Shulkin leaving and his replacement, but what I didn't know is that the president had been considering me. He hadn't spoken to many people about it, and I don't believe he had seriously discussed it with Kelly.

The first time I ever heard anything about it was at Mar-a-Lago. I was sitting outside, and suddenly, the door opened, and General Kelly came out, and I heard him yell, "Dr. Jackson."

I heard somebody say, "What?"

He said, "Where's Ronny?"

They said, "He's here somewhere."

When I heard my name, I hopped up. As I turned the corner, General Kelly poked his head out and said, "Hey, Ronny, get in here. The president wants you in on this conversation."

I thought, *What the heck's going on?* I had no idea.

I went in, they pulled a chair up, and the president said, "Sit down, Ronny." The president, General Kelly, and House Speaker Paul Ryan were seated at the table, and they were discussing VA issues.

Paul Ryan was talking when I came in. I'd probably met Paul Ryan in passing, but he didn't know who I was. When I walked into the room, Speaker Ryan stood up and said, "Admiral." I said hello, shook his hand, and sat down.

As I said before, the president and I talked numerous times about veterans' issues and the Department of Defense, and the president knew that I had an interest in it. He trusted my judgment, and he knew he'd get a straight answer from me.

Right away, the president asked me, "Ronny, so what do you think about David? Is David doing a good job? What do you think?"

I said, "Yes, sir, I think he's doing a good job." General Kelly was chiming in a little bit too. He wasn't saying David *wasn't* doing a good job, but I could tell that's what the discussion had been about before I got there.

The president then said, "Paul, you want to fix the VA? I can tell you how to fix the VA."

Speaker Ryan said, "Sir, I'm all ears. What do you got?"

He said, "If you want to fix the VA, you put the admiral in charge of it," and he pointed at me.

Speaker Ryan looked confused and said, "All right, sir," and was just kind of smiling and shaking his head in agreement.

The president said, "No, I'm serious. The admiral understands the VA better than anyone, and he'll do a great job."

General Kelly was like, "Whoa, whoa, whoa, I think we're getting a little ahead of ourselves here. The admiral has some obligations he's got to fill in the military before he can consider something like that."

Immediately, Kelly was trying to back the president off the idea. I didn't think anything of it, to be honest with you. I just laughed about it too. Then the president said a couple of other times, "No, I'm telling you, if you want to fix it, you put the admiral in charge."

We discussed a few other issues not related to the VA. Then the meeting was over, and I got up and walked out. I did not think he was serious; I thought he was flattering me; I thought the president was patting me on the back about what a good job I was doing. I didn't think it was a serious consideration. I didn't.

In hindsight, it was. He was dead serious. Looking back at how Kelly responded to it, it was apparently the first time he had heard it. He, however, didn't waste any time trying to shut it down.

The meeting came and went, a few weeks went by, and we were on the plane, flying from Mar-a-Lago, back to DC. The president was walking down the main passageway on the plane. He walked past my medical space, which was right next to his office at the front of the plane, and he said, "Doc, come on up front. I have something to talk to you about."

I said, "Yes, sir."

I got up and followed him into his office on Air Force One, and he said, "Sit down." So, I did.

"I need you to do me a favor," the president said.

I said, "Yes, sir, what do you need?"

He said, "I want you to be a member of my cabinet. I want you to be my VA secretary."

I said, "Sir?"

"Well, you can do it, right?" said the president.

I responded, "Well, hell yeah, I can do it, but where did this come from?"

"Ronny, you're the right guy for the job. You care about the veterans. You and I have conversations all the time about the veterans; you're motivated by the right reasons and not controlled by special interests or lobbies or influenced by those just interested in propping up the bloated VA budget. You're always concerned about what's best for the veterans. You have the right attitude, the right approach; you're an admiral in the military, you're about to retire and be a veteran, you're a leader who gets it. I can trust you, and I know you're always going to do the right thing for the vets, and you're the right guy for the job."

I said, "Well, thank you, sir. I appreciate it, and I am honored you would consider me for something like this."

"Here's what I want you to do: you go home and talk to Jane about it, and if you're on board and if she supports it, then let's make this happen!"

I said, "Yes, sir."

Air Force One landed, we boarded Marine One, and we flew back to the White House. General Kelly and a handful of senior staff were on the helicopter as well. When we landed on the South Lawn of the White House, everyone headed across the lawn to the West Wing except for me and the president. We headed into the White House. The president said good night, got on the elevator, and went up to his residence. I didn't go back to my office. Instead, I walked straight over to the West Wing to catch General Kelly before he went home.

I walked into his office, and I said, "Sir, I just want to make you aware of something."

He said, "What is it, Ronny?"

"The president spoke to me tonight, and he wants to nominate me for VA secretary."

"What?"

"Yes, sir, he talked to me about it on the plane."

"Ronny, you don't want to do this." And he immediately started trying to talk me out of it.

I said, "Why not?"

"Ronny, I don't want to see this town chew up and spit out another good man. I couldn't recommend in good conscience that anybody take that job right now; you don't want to do this, believe me. It's not going to be good, it's not what you want to do, and it's just going to be hard on you and your family."

I trusted him 100 percent. I thought he was looking out for my best interests, but I was really leaning towards accepting the president's offer anyway.

He said, "I'm telling you, Ronny, you're a good friend of mine.... I don't want to see you do this. I don't want to see your family put through this. You definitely should not do this, Ronny."

I told him I'd go and talk to my wife. He said, "All right, let's get together and talk about this tomorrow. He could tell I was going to do it. As I was about to walk out, he said, "Ronny, if you do decide to do this, we have to do it the right way. We should slow-roll the whole thing. Let's leak out to the press that you might be the nominee and see what happens. This way, we can shore up any perceived weakness in the nomination and make sure we get you confirmed. We also need to wait until you get promoted. Your nomination for your second star is in the Senate now and should be confirmed any day. Let's not mess that up. Let's get you promoted, and then we can move forward. We can have someone designated as the "acting secretary" in the meantime."

I said, "Okay," and I went home and talked to Jane about it. Jane has always been behind me no matter what I decide to do, and this was no different. She realized it would be stressful and difficult and that the family might be drawn into it as well. It didn't matter. She was with me 110 percent!

The more I thought about it, the more I wanted to do it. I was a little bummed that General Kelly was trying to talk me out of it, but I thought he was doing it for the right reasons—because he was worried about me. By the next morning, I had decided that I was absolutely going to do it. I was in my office that morning when the president came down the elevator on his way to the Oval Office. I was standing in the doorway of my office and told him, "Good morning, Mr. President," as he got off the elevator. He said, "Walk with me, we need to talk."

We walked down the West Colonnade, and he asked, "Are we going to do this?"

I said, "Yes, sir, we're gonna do it."

He said, "All right, good. That's what I like to hear. You go get your ducks in a row, come back over to the office, I'll grab Kelly, and we'll figure out what we're going to do."

I said, "Sounds great, sir. Also, wanted to let you know I spoke to General Kelly about it, and he thinks we should slow-roll it a little. That we should leak it out and then wait a few weeks to make it official. He thinks…"

The president stopped walking and interjected, "Wait? No, we're not waiting. What does he want to wait for? We're going to do this today."

I tried to elaborate, "Well, sir, I think he thinks we should name an acting secretary and take some time to figure out…."

He jumped in again and said, "No, we are going to do this today. Boom, boom, Shulkin is out, and you're in," he said as he slapped the back of his hand into the palm of his other hand.

I said, "Well, sir, General Kelly thinks…"

He stopped me again and said, "Doc, General Kelly knows this is my decision, not his, right?"

I said, "Oh, yes, sir. He knows that. He just…"

"Ronny," he said, "we're going to do this today. Boom, Boom, Shulkin is out, and you're in," he repeated. "Don't worry about it. You let me handle General Kelly. Go do what you have to do this morning, get over to my office, and let's get this done," he said.

I turned around, and I went back, but I didn't go back to my office. Instead, I went through the Palm Room, walked outside past the Press Briefing Room, through the visitors' entrance of the West Wing Lobby, and directly into General Kelly's office.

General Kelly was there. I said, "Sir, I know we talked about this yesterday. I've decided I'm going to do this, but we've got a little bit of a problem with your plan to roll this out."

He said, "Well, I wish you wouldn't do this, Ronny. But what's the problem?"

"Well, I talked to the president this morning, and he is planning to make the announcement today."

He said, "What? No, we need to wait."

"I told him exactly what you said, but he's convinced it's best to do it right away. He's adamant we're doing it now."

"Doc, you let me handle the president; I'll talk to him, and I'll take care of it."

So this was funny; the president had just told me, "You let me handle Kelly," and Kelly had just told me, "You let me handle the president." I figured I would go back to my office and let the two of them work it out. I could go back over shortly and find out what the plan was.

I got busy in my office, several hours had passed, it was already early afternoon, and I hadn't heard anything. I assumed Kelly won the fight and managed to convince the president that we should slow-roll it a little bit. But about that time, Hope Hicks and Sarah Sanders walked into my office, and they had these big grins on their faces. They said, "Congratulations!"

As far as I knew, nobody even knew about it except for me, General Kelly, and the president. I hadn't told anybody about it; I hadn't mentioned it to anybody except for Jane. So I said, "Oh, did the president tell you guys that he's thinking about making me the VA secretary?"

They looked a little confused and said, "What?"

I asked again, "Did he tell you that he might be nominating me as the VA secretary soon?"

The expression on their faces turned to a slightly concerned look, and Hope said, "Ronny, have you not been over there?"

I said, "No."

Sarah said, "Well, Ronny, you better get over there. They're working on the tweet right now and are gonna announce it in thirty minutes."

I jumped up out of my chair, ran over to the Oval Office, and sure enough, the president was sitting at the desk drafting the announcement. Dan Scavino was there, and he was already putting together a tweet for the president's approval. The vice president, General Kelly, Sarah, and Hope were there, as well as several others, such as Nick Ayers, the vice president's chief of staff, Sean Doocey, the director of presidential personnel, and Shealah Craighead, the president's photographer. It was quite the crowd, and everyone was congratulating me, patting me on the back, and affectionately calling me "Mr. Secretary."

Dan handed the president a printed copy of the draft tweet. The president edited it, then handed it back to Dan. Meanwhile, General Kelly stepped out to call Secretary David Shulkin and let him know he was being fired. Dan returned with the tweet for final approval. The president looked it over, signed it, handed it to me, and said,

"Welcome to the big league, Doc!" And that was it; it was a done deal. With that tweet, the president fired the secretary, appointed an acting, and named me as his nominee for the next secretary of veterans affairs. It was an exciting day, and one I will never forget!

What I didn't know is that there was a group of individuals spread throughout the government who had already decided who they wanted to serve in the role of secretary of veterans affairs. This was my first exposure to the "deep state" of government, and these people believed that President Trump was not capable of picking his own cabinet and that it was their "duty to the country" to do that for him. As I mentioned, everyone knew that David Shulkin was on his way out, and this group of individuals had already decided that Robert Wilkie should take his place. They had been planning for months and were just waiting on the decision to get rid of Shulkin. The plan was to fire Shulkin, make Wilkie the acting secretary, get him some face time with the president, get some wins under his belt, and then convince the president he should be the nominee. The problem was President Trump wasn't a part of all of this, and they had no idea that President Trump was going to nominate me and screw up their plan. Now, nothing against Secretary Wilkie, I actually think he did a great job as VA secretary, but at the time, President Trump didn't know him that well and was not going to make him the nominee. When the president revealed that I was going to be his nominee, that is when all hell broke loose, and they had to figure out a way to undo that and get me out of the way.

They considered me a loose cannon who they had no control or influence over. They were terrified I would answer directly to the president, which, by the way, is the way it is supposed to work for cabinet secretaries. Wilkie, on the other hand, had strong existing relationships with many of the stakeholders. He was a longtime Senate staffer and had worked closely with many members of the Senate Veterans' Affairs committee. This was the committee that would be responsible for my confirmation hearing as the nominee. In fact, he had been a senior advisor to Senator Thom Tillis, on the committee, and worked for many years with the chairman, Johnny Isakson, and the ranking member, Jon Tester. When he left his job as a congressional staffer, he went to work in senior positions in the Pentagon and worked closely with the secretary of defense, General Mattis, and General John Kelly, who would eventually be the White House chief of staff during this time. There were many others working in the Department of Veterans Affairs, the Senate, the Department of Defense, and the West Wing of the White House who were also behind the scenes working to get Wilkie nominated. Everyone had something personal to gain.

I am not bitter about it, and I understand how it all works. Everyone wants to have influence with people in powerful positions, certainly if they may have something to offer them down the road, and especially if they control a $260 billion/year budget. Unfortunately, I thought most of these people were working on behalf of the president to get me confirmed, but they weren't. I didn't figure any of this out until after I had withdrawn my nomination. It was obvious to me, however, just before I withdrew my nomination, that many of the Republicans who should have been fostering my nomination and helping me in the fight with the Democrats and the mainstream media were quietly looking the other way.

They couldn't just come out and openly oppose me because they worked for the president, and I was the president's pick. Even if it meant destroying me in the process, they had to figure out a way to get rid of me. Looking back now, that's why General Kelly was having that conversation with me; Kelly knew how this was going to play out, which is why he started this aggressive process to try to talk me out of it. Even while I was in the nomination process and before any accusations came out, Kelly approached me a couple of times, and so did his deputy chief of staff, a guy named Zach Fuentes, who turned out to be a real snake in the grass. They would say, "It's not too late to back out; we can still pull your nomination paperwork."

Everything was going perfectly, so I was confused. Why were they having this conversation with me? The overwhelming consensus was that I would be confirmed. There was no indication whatsoever that I wasn't going to breeze through this confirmation hearing, yet they were still saying it wasn't too late: "If you want to back out, we can make that happen. Just let us take care of it." I thought, *Why would I back out now? Screw that! Everything is going great.*

The day the president nominated me by sending out a tweet, General Kelly said, "Ronny, you need to resign your commission as a physician to the president immediately. You can't do that job and be a nominee for secretary of the VA. The nomination process is a full-time job, so you need to give me your resignation paperwork tomorrow."

I said, "Yes, sir."

I wrote up a resignation letter resigning as the president's physician and turned the job over to Dr. Sean Conley, who would immediately become the acting physician to the president. I resigned as the president's physician the very next day because General Kelly had told me to. It turns out I didn't need to; I kind of regret doing that now because I think the real reason was to get me out of the inner circle of the White House while they figured out how to sink my nomination.

However, General Kelly was right about the fact that the nomination process is a full-time job.

I immediately moved out of my office in the White House and moved into a big office over in the Eisenhower Executive Office Building (EEOB). I was also assigned a large staff of all new people. My new staff was a hybrid from the VA and White House Office of Cabinet Affairs. I was getting briefed every day from seven o'clock in the morning until ten at night. I was getting back-to-back briefs on everything you could think of related to the VA. I would finish a brief, open the door to let them out, and there'd be five more people standing in the hallway to come in and brief me. This continued all day long. I was drinking from a fire hose! It was brutal. I barely even got to eat.

In the evening, we would have "murder boards" or mock hearings, where they'd set up the Indian Treaty Room in the EEOB to look like the Senate hearing room. They would have people familiar with all the issues come in and act as mock senators and drill me on questions to get ready for the hearing.

Initially, those who wanted me to fail, including General Kelly and many people in the Veterans' Affairs Committee, thought I would fall on my sword from an experience and leadership standpoint. I think they thought that I wasn't going to be able to pull it off, that I was going to look like I couldn't do the job during my confirmation hearing, and I wouldn't get confirmed. But that wasn't happening. I was working my butt off. I met with every single senator on the Veterans' Affairs Committee—I also met with senate leadership, my Texas senators, and a few others. I met with over twenty-five of them getting ready for this.

One of the bright spots in the whole process was when I met with Lindsey Graham. Lindsey wasn't on the Veterans' Affairs Committee. But he was a well-respected leader in the Senate, and I asked him if he would be willing to introduce me during my upcoming Senate confirmation hearing. We had met several times before, and I really liked him. He not only readily agreed but thought it would be even better if we could get a Senate Democrat to also introduce me. So, he reached out to Joe Manchin and set up a meeting for me. I had never met Manchin. But once I did, I really liked the guy. He also agreed to introduce me. Later, when the accusations came out, Lindsey aggressively defended me but Manchin, being a Democrat, had to back away and stay quiet. Lindsey went to bat for me; that guy defended me to the hilt. He and President Trump were on TV supporting me all the time; those guys never left me.

I approached the entire confirmation process with the attitude that I was an active-duty navy rear admiral, an emergency medicine physician, and had worked directly for three presidents. I had everything I needed to get through this process and be the best VA secretary the department has ever seen. I studied my ass off and knew more about the VA than just about anyone I spoke to. I would go in to these meetings with the senators, and they would ask me a question about something. I'd then answer the question in great detail, tie it to other issues, elaborate, and discuss the specifics of the issue to their state. Word got around to everybody, "This guy's killing it, he really knows the issues, he's working hard and taking this seriously, and he's doing a great job in the mock hearings."

I think they thought to themselves, *We're going to have to confirm this guy. He's going to get up there for his confirmation hearing, on TV in front of the American public, and he is going to inspire confidence. This guy is going to do such a great job that we are going to have no choice but to confirm him!*

I think that, at that point, they decided to go with plan B: destroy me on a personal level. And that's exactly what they tried to do.

Everything was going great. I passed the extensive FBI background investigation that every cabinet member must have, my financial disclosure information was completed and had been reviewed by all the committee lawyers, and my nomination went over to the Senate. I was officially the nominee. My FBI investigation was officially briefed to the chairman of the committee, Johnny Isakson, and the ranking member, Jon Tester. They were told it was completely clean, and I passed with no concerns. I was moving through the process at a rapid pace and had cleared all the significant hurdles. The only thing left was to sit for my confirmation hearing, and that was scheduled for the following week. I was doing extremely well, and everyone thought it was a slam dunk from that point forward. In addition to having just passed an extensive FBI security background investigation, I had held a Top Secret/SCI Yankee White security clearance for the past twelve years at the White House. I had been cleared at the absolute highest level of government. I worked directly, one-on-one, with three US presidents. I literally had every aspect of my life looked into for decades and NEVER had one negative comment or finding. Despite this, Senator Jon Tester decided to propagate unsubstantiated lies generated by a couple of disgruntled prior employees of mine. He did this knowing they were untrue and only days after the FBI had told him there was nothing in my background of concern. He and his staff convinced these individuals that they would stay anonymous and could say anything they wanted in an effort to damage me and the nomination process. Jon Tester is the epitome of a slimy, disgusting politician, and he used these hapless vindictive idiots as his pawns.

So they got together, conspired, and started the process of trying to tear me down. At that point, I had been at the White House for twelve years and had managed hundreds of people. I was in a leadership position the entire time I was there, either as the deputy director, the director of the White House Medical Unit, the physician to the president, or some combination of those duties. As the officer in charge, I was always signing people's fitness and performance reports. I was doing their awards and deciding who got to stay and who had to go when their military tours were up at the White House.

There were a few disgruntled employees, people who didn't pull their weight, and it came time for them to leave. They asked if they could stay for another couple of years, and I said, "No, we need you to move on and do whatever's next. We're going to bring somebody else in." It was unavoidable, but I made a few enemies as a result. I don't regret this. Someone had to make these types of decisions, and unfortunately, it was part of my job. My job was an absolute no-fail job. My job was to take care of the president of the United States and to keep him alive under any and all circumstances, no matter what happened. So, did I hold people to high standards? You bet I did. Did a few people end up having to move on because they weren't pulling their weight? Yes, you bet they did.

In addition to a few employees who left a little disgruntled, I had three that I could not easily get rid of because of the unique relationships they had in their jobs. These were individuals who still worked for me but had a connection with the vice president or president that made it difficult to fire them. Looking back, I should have acted and removed them anyway. They were driven by jealousy, plagued with insecurity, and had a real negative impact on team cohesiveness.

Chief among this group was Kevin O'Connor. He was Biden's physician the full eight years that Biden was vice president. During this same time, I was the appointed physician to the president for President Obama, the director of the White House Medical Unit, and his boss. He and I arrived at the White House at essentially the same time, and he was senior to me in rank. As a result, he was always resentful of the fact that I was promoted to take care of the president and that he ended up being responsible for the vice president. He spent the entire time he was at the White House trying to undermine my authority behind closed doors. I didn't appreciate it but had to tolerate it due to the fact that he developed a close relationship with then-Vice President Biden. He was best known for his inappropriate sense of humor; however, his relationship with Biden protected him.

On January 20, 2017, when Biden was no longer VP, O'Connor left the White House, ultimately retired from the army, and got a job working at George Washington University.

Once it was publicly released that President Trump was nominating me as the secretary of veterans affairs, O'Connor, Jen Peña, and a few others began a coordinated effort to attack me.

Peña had worked closely with O'Connor during the last year of the Obama administration and served as the backup physician for Vice President Biden much of the time. She stayed on at the end of the Obama/Biden administration and continued in the role of the physician for the vice president for Vice President Pence. At the time, I didn't understand the influence Dr. O'Connor had on her, and I liked and trusted her. I was actually responsible for asking her to stay on as Pence's physician. It became obvious later that she saw herself as next in line to be the physician for the president and thought that would happen if somehow I were no longer in the role. We got along most of the time, but she grew to hate me when I had to step in and override a few bad medical decisions she was making. I was an emergency medicine physician with decades of experience, and she was an internal medicine physician with significantly less experience. A decision was made that I did not clinically agree with, and I overrode it and changed the plan. It was nothing personal and strictly in the best interest of the patient, but unfortunately, she took it very personally and never really got over it. I know this because she talked about it frequently to other members of the White House Medical Unit. This incident, along with all the drama she brought to the team surrounding my nomination, eventually led the Pence team to lose confidence in her ability, and ultimately, they had to get rid of her. They made it clear they no longer wanted her to be responsible for their care or travel with their team. They essentially fired her. Once she could no longer perform her duties in caring for the vice president and his team, the army decided it was time for her to leave the unit.

The role she and Dr. O'Connor played in pushing the false accusations regarding me to the Senate was revealed when she broke down in tears in the medical unit just before her departure. I was not present, but several members reported that she was upset she was having to leave and blamed it on Dr. O'Connor.

She made the comment in front of multiple members of the unit, "This is not right. I'm taking the fall for all of this! This wasn't even my idea. This was all Kevin O'Connor's idea." She told one member of the unit that during my confirmation process, Kevin O'Connor coordinated with her and a few others and discussed ways to undermine my nomination. Apparently, they wanted to get together on their stories and decide who was going to say what. They also had a physical therapist, who was essentially President Obama's massage therapist, involved. This individual worked for me as well during the Obama administration and did not like me because he felt like I had too much control over his access to the president.

So, they talked about it, came up with their story, coordinated who was going to say what, and made sure all their stories were the same.

Then somehow, I assume using their legislative affairs contacts from the Obama administration, they set up a meeting with Senator Tester's staff on the Senate Veterans' Affairs Committee and flat out lied. None of it was under oath, and they were assured that they would remain completely anonymous. Tester's team did everything they could to encourage them to lie, misrepresent, and manipulate their stories in order to do the maximum amount of damage to my nomination. Then, Senator Tester, without ever asking me about the accusations, without making any effort whatsoever to verify what was being said, released it to CNN and MSNBC as if it were verified and factual. Tester's team knew the source of the information was unreliable and from disgruntled former employees of mine who were motivated by their personal dislike for me and had an axe to grind. They didn't care. This was a scorched-earth political hit job, and all they cared about was generating the necessary headlines to stop me. They were more than happy to use these pawns that had worked with me in the Obama/Biden administration to help them get the job done. Here's the kicker. You know who President Biden's physician is right now? Kevin O'Connor. Are you surprised? I must admit, I am not; he probably still fits in quite well there.

Our government is full of bad people, both elected and unelected, who have no problem lying if it is in their own best interest. Tester is an absolute disgrace and represents everything that is wrong with our government. He will say or do anything if he thinks it is in his best interest politically. It is corrupt and dishonest elected officials like him who drove me to run for office myself.

As I mentioned before, Tester knew Wilkie. Everybody involved did—with a few possible exceptions, it was the Republicans and the Democrats on the Veterans' Affairs Committee in the Senate who wanted him there. They thought he was somebody they could manipulate and have influence over, and they knew I wasn't. They hated the fact I was a Trump guy. So it was a win-win for them. They got to tear somebody down who was close to Trump and do it while trying to get the person whom they wanted appointed to his cabinet.

When the accusations came out, I was at the White House. Everyone was calling and texting, "Are you watching the news? Do you see what's going on?" Most people in the White House were legitimately shocked by it. Even those who had been intimately involved in politics for decades said they couldn't remember the press ever coming after someone so aggressively. Looking back now, I think the one exception was General Kelly. I don't think he was surprised at all. Of course, he acted like it was a horrible thing, and he was super pissed off about it, but looking back now, I think he knew it was coming.

I don't think he was personally involved in it, but he definitely looked the other way and let it happen. Unfortunately, he screwed me on many fronts, and one of the things he did as soon as the lies came out was convince me that we needed to request that the Department of the Defense Office of the Inspector General start an investigation to clear my name. He said we should have the Senate Armed Services Committee do this since my promotion was still in their committee. He told me that because of the high-profile nature of my role as the nominee for a cabinet position, it would only take a few weeks for them to look into the accusations and clear my name. "We'll have this done in three weeks: we'll have the investigation completed, the truth out there, your name cleared, we'll get you promoted, and we'll get this nomination back on track." Turned out to be horrible advice, and I think it was part of the follow-on plan to make sure I kept my mouth shut and didn't publicly fight back against the accusations.

Initially, I thought, *We want to ask the DoD IG?* I didn't trust the IG; who does? They're a bunch of partisan hacks in just about every department and certainly in DoD. My only experience with the DoD IG is that you're guilty until proven innocent. They were out to try to destroy people because that's how they made a name for themselves. So I was hesitant about it, but I trusted General Kelly. I reluctantly said, "Okay, let's do it." General Kelly took care of the rest.

As I have said before, I respect General Kelly's service to our country and all the great things he did while in the military. But I think he and many others embedded in the Trump administration thought it was somehow their "patriotic duty" to protect the country from what they viewed as President Trump's dangerous and reckless approach. Nothing could be further from the truth. President Trump was the one who was actively saving the country, and these are the people who represent the biggest threat to our democracy, our republic, and our national security. The people get to decide who makes decisions on their behalf, not a few self-appointed, unelected "patriots."

When the lies and leftist stories came out against me, Trump was pissed. He said, "You tell me what you want to do. If you want to fight this, we will fight it!" He was encouraging me to stay in the fight, and initially, I did. However, I found out later from others in the West Wing that the president was also getting information when

I wasn't in the room. He had Kelly and all of Kelly's crew in there, telling him that my nomination was dead in the water; there was no way it was going to go. He was getting mixed messages. They were spinning it in a way that they thought would ultimately get him to back away from his support for me, which he never did. He wanted me to fight it, and he wanted to be in the fight with me.

If I had said, "Sir, I'm not backing down. I'm staying in this to the very end," he would have stood with me to the very end.

Once I withdrew my nomination, and after Kelly had talked me into supporting the notion of a DoD investigation, Zach Fuentes, Kelly's deputy, inserted himself into the whole process. I initially thought he was a friend and that he was working hard to help me get everything closed out. Turns out that was not the case. I found out from numerous sources before I finally left the White House that he and Kelly were doing me harm behind closed doors. Their actions and what they were saying were dragging me down instead of helping me out. They were also working with a few individuals in White House Counsel to slow-roll things and drag out this "investigation." I later realized this was all a way to keep me quiet and in my box.

Throughout this entire process, from the day the accusations came out until I retired and left active duty, I was unable to defend myself. I was told by General Kelly, the White House Counsel's Office, and the navy that I was not allowed to talk about the accusations. I was not allowed to speak to the press, and I had to keep my mouth shut because there was an active DoD investigation. That's the other reason Kelly wanted an investigation open: once they opened the DoD IG investigation, I was muted. I couldn't talk to the press; I couldn't defend myself. I couldn't go out to the media and say, "That's ridiculous." I was an active-duty navy rear admiral, so the navy was still able to control me to some extent. In addition to that, I was an appointed assistant to the president, so I had presidential privilege that had to be taken into consideration. The White House lawyers in the White House Counsel's Office told me I couldn't say anything either. I had to spend money out of my own pocket to hire a lawyer as a result of all of this. It became obvious very quickly that the DoD IG had an agenda, and they didn't really care about the facts. The acting DoD IG was a former Clinton and Obama appointee and pretty obviously a liberal. They were using me to establish precedent allowing them access to anyone who worked in the White House who happened to be on active duty. They wanted the authority to come into the White House and interview people, get documents, and have full rein of the place. Just another example of the government being weaponized for political reasons.

Unfortunately, for over a week, the stories just kept coming. The same lies and accusations were on TV constantly—every channel you turned on. They were able to run with whatever crazy accusations they wanted, and I just had to suck it up and keep my mouth shut. It was very obvious they were going to keep pushing this garbage until they reached critical mass and I decided to withdraw my nomination.

Ultimately, I did decide to withdraw, but I did so because I began to realize that I was not only fighting the Democrats and the mainstream media, but also key Republicans. They were supposed to be fostering my nomination and helping me, but instead were quietly looking away and letting the attacks happen. I also legitimately began to feel like President Trump's agenda for the veterans was becoming part of the story and it was undermining the great things he was doing and had planned for our veterans. I won't lie, I lived in one of the most liberal counties in the country, and it made things very difficult for my wife and kids. Jane couldn't even leave the house because of all the press camped out at the bottom of our driveway. My kids were getting harassed at school, and my parents were getting bombarded with phone calls from the most disgusting elements of the liberal media.

Eventually, I said to myself, *You know what, I'm finished with this crap.* At that point, I went to talk to Sarah Sanders. I was sitting in Sarah's office, and I spoke to her, and she said, "Ronny, it's really up to you. You know we back you, the president is leaving this up to you; if you want out, if you've had enough, he'll back you withdrawing your nomination, and if you do want to stay in the fight, he'll back you until the bitter end, and you know that."

I said, "I know that. But this is too much for my family, and I don't feel like I'm getting the support I need outside of the Oval Office. So I'm going to withdraw my nomination." I drafted up my resignation, gave it to her, we let the president know, and she released it to the press.

The president was adamant about doing anything and everything he could to help me. But key Republicans were not in my corner, and at the time, I didn't even know who was on my team and who was trying to kill me.

Now, many people in the White House *were* busting their butts to help me. The press team, Sarah Sanders, Hogan Gidley, all the legislative affairs team, the presidential personnel team, and many of the transition staffers from the VA—those people were definitely in my corner. They were working hard to make sure that I had everything I needed to make it through this and to fight back, but no one had ever seen the press just come after somebody as aggressively as they came after me. Unfortunately, it has happened multiple times since then to other nominees. I tell people all the time: I got "Kavanaugh'd" before

Kavanaugh. I was the warm-up; I was the pregame. I just didn't know it at the time.

From that point forward, I was Trump's guy. That meant I also had the "Never Trumpers" against me from then on—and they were in every branch of government. Many of them appeared to support the Trump agenda. But behind the scenes, they never stopped working against him. Initially, even President Trump didn't realize how extensive this network was. He assumed early on, and rightfully so, that everyone in the executive branch worked for him as president and would support his agenda. That was NOT the case. They slowed him down in the beginning, but thankfully, he figured out what was going on and was able to do more for this country than anyone before him. I, like many Americans, can't help but wonder what he would have been capable of with the support he was due.

I think even President Trump would say one of the biggest mistakes he made coming into office was assuming that everyone who worked for the Executive Office of the President and the cabinet-level departments, including the Department of Justice, Department of Defense, Department of Treasury, Department of Veterans Affairs, and so on, effectively worked for him. Their job was to help him with his agenda and help him get things done as the president. That's the way it's supposed to work. These are supposed to be career, nonpartisan employees working for the president.

However, in the case of President Trump, he had to deal with this deep-state mentality that was like a cancer in these departments. It was disgusting. I had friends who worked in the Department of Justice who said their offices' leadership refused to put the president's picture on the wall. When Obama was gone, they took Obama's picture down, and they left a blank spot on the wall where the president's official photo usually hangs. They wore anti-Trump T-shirts to work sometimes, and they got away with it. Things you would have been fired for in other administrations were now tolerated because of this deep-state garbage. And the DoD was as bad as anybody.

Going back to General Kelly, I think he was a mixed bag. I think he wanted to see the president succeed, but he also felt like he was the check and balance for what he perceived as over the top. Kelly would use his position and authority to throttle things back or limit what the president was seeing or doing. This was all being done behind the scenes. It should piss all Americans off. President Trump was kicking ass, and he was doing what the country needed him to do. He was draining the damn swamp, and that's why people were freaking out. That's why the deep state was born, because the deep state is the swamp. That's where they thrive and live and where they hold their power and authority.

President Trump wasn't doing anything reckless; he wasn't doing anything dangerous. He wasn't doing anything that the American people didn't want him to do. He was doing what he was elected to do. That was contrary to good order in the swamp, and that's why these people rose to think that they had to be the saviors and limit the damage he could potentially do to the establishment. That's what it was about: salvaging the establishment.

Once I had withdrawn my nomination, I didn't know what I was going to do. Remember the day I got nominated? Kelly told me to resign as the physician to the president, so I didn't have a role at the White House anymore. The president assumed I was going to come back to my previous job as his personal physician. But I had done that for a long time, and I was looking for something new. The president asked me, "What are you going to do? Are you going to come back and be my doc again?"

I said, "No, sir. I don't think that's the best thing to do, and I'm going to retire soon."

He said, "I don't want you to leave; I would like for you to stay around. We want to promote you to assistant to the president and make you the chief medical advisor. Everyone wants you to stay and would like for you to work on some policy issues for us."

I said, "That's great," because I wanted a break, and I wanted to do something different. I was a little burned out on the clinical stuff after doing it for fourteen years. So, to get a job as assistant to the president and the chief medical advisor, and work on policy instead, was a nice opportunity. I would also have the distinct honor of being the first-ever appointed chief medical advisor—a role that the White House desperately needed and, oddly enough, the role now filled by Dr. Anthony Fauci. I am *very* sorry!

I started working on policy; I worked on the opioid crisis, issues involving the Indian Health Service, VA healthcare, telehealth utilization, pharmaceutical pricing, and a host of other issues. Kelly had told me to "stay away from the press, not travel with the president or anything for a while; just lay low and let this DoD IG run its course. Just give it three to four weeks, and we're going to have this all knocked out, get your name cleared, get you promoted, and then we'll go from there."

So, for three to four weeks, I worked from home as much as possible, kept a low profile, and when I went to the White House, I avoided the press. The funny thing is I ended up walking past the press several times, and every time, someone would stop me and tell me that they were really sorry about what was happening to me and that they really appreciated all the times I had been there for them on overseas trips. If a member of the press corps got sick on an overseas trip, I was always there to check them out and get them the medication and care they needed. So, this was a really strange situation. These were the people who were tearing me down every day, now going out of their way to tell me they didn't believe what they were reporting and thanking me for taking care of them.

I was just really disgruntled after the nomination fell through. For months and months, I was getting more and more bitter. I thought, *I hate this place; I hate DC. It's disgusting, it's a swamp, it's a sewer; I want out of this damn place. I can't stand it here.* I wanted to go back home to Texas!

I could get a job making way more money than I was making in the military: sitting on boards, working as a consultant, and maybe doing an occasional shift in the emergency department. I would work fewer hours, too, and not have to put up with any of the garbage I had just been subjected to. I was excited about it, and so was Jane. But then, as time went on, I became more uneasy about how things were closing out.

I didn't regret that I withdrew my nomination because I really believed it was the right thing to do, and I also knew the job would have been very frustrating. It's an unenviable job in some regards because it's such a massive bureaucracy that it's almost impossible to make meaningful change in the short period of time that most secretaries have in the role. That said, it is a very important job, and I would have been very good at it.

I didn't like what they did to me during the nomination process, and every day, I saw more and more evidence that our country was going to hell. I had seen the deep state firsthand, and they were continuing to go after Trump relentlessly. I was especially terrified at the way the mainstream media was willingly being used as a weapon for the Left. I thought, *Our country is really in trouble.* Something needed to be done.

7.

It was early October 2019, and I turned the TV on as I was getting dressed for work. It was six o'clock in the morning. I saw that Congressman Mac Thornberry wasn't going to run for reelection. He represented the Thirteenth Congressional District in Texas. I grew up in the Nineteenth Congressional District, about forty-five minutes from his district, in the base of the Texas Panhandle. Thornberry had been the congressman there for twenty-six years, and it was now going to be an open seat.

When I saw that, I had an epiphany. I thought, *Wow! Thornberry isn't running again, and this is going to be an open seat. The economy is booming, and President Trump is about to get reelected to a second term. And I am about to put my retirement paperwork in and move back to Texas. This is an unbelievable opportunity for me to get in the fight and do something about what is going on in our country. Not complain about it, not bitch about, but DO something about it!* At the time, I thought, like most Americans, that Trump was destined to get another four years. Everything was going extremely well, and all the indicators that decide if a president gets reelected were overwhelmingly in his favor. I realized that if I got into Congress, I could have unusual influence as a freshman congressman based on my existing relationship with the White House. Well, the part of the equation about having Trump in the White House didn't exactly work out, but I feel like I have an even more important role now trying to stop the insanity from the current White House. And by the way, he won!

As I said, I saw this as an unusual trifecta of circumstances and an opportunity to make a difference. I went to work at the White House that day, and by the end of the day, I didn't even see it as an opportunity anymore; I saw it as an obligation and a duty. I had been uneasy about things ever since I withdrew my nomination for VA secretary, and I didn't know where it was going to ultimately lead me. Now I knew: this was it. This was where I was supposed to be, and this was what I was supposed to do! I kept thinking about it all day at work, and by the end of the day, I walked into the Oval Office unannounced, and I told the president, "Sir, I'm leaving."

He said, "What do you mean you're leaving?" He thought something was wrong, maybe with my family. "What's wrong?"

I said, "Nothing, sir. I'm going to run for office."

He said, "You're going to run for office? For what?"

I said, "I'm going to run for Congress. I'm running for the Thirteenth Congressional District in Texas."

He called out to his executive assistant and said, "Molly, get Brian on the phone." Brian Jack was his political director. Luckily, I had seen Brian when I was walking over to the Oval Office, and I had told him I was thinking about doing it, and he'd said, "Wow, that's awesome."

About that time, Brian walked into the outer Oval Office, and the president said, "Brian, get in here. Ronny wants to run for office."

Brian said, "I know, sir."

President Trump said, "Where are you running?" I told him the Texas Thirteenth Congressional District. He said, "Who's currently in that seat, Brian? Ronny said his name is Thornberry?"

Brian said, "Yes, sir. He's retiring."

The president said, "Well, Ronny would be great, especially if this is going to be an open seat. Who else is running?" They didn't know who all would be running at the time, but there was already a crowd of people saying they were going to, including Thornberry's hand-picked successor.

The president asked, "Are any of them Trump people?"

Brian said, "Well, sir, they're all Trump people in that part of Texas—that's Trump country—but they're not Trump people like Ronny."

The president said, "I've heard enough. It sounds like Ronny is the right man for the job! Good luck, Ronny."

The president was excited about me running. It just so happens that during all this, energy secretary, fellow Texan, and former governor of the great state of Texas, Rick Perry walked into the outer Oval Office with his wife, Anita, and their new grandbaby. They had just had a little grandson. Secretary Perry was getting ready to retire as the secretary of energy, and they were there to get a departure picture with the president. When he walked in and heard what was going on, he and Anita were all in. So, there I was, standing in the Oval Office with President Trump, Governor Perry, and Brian Jack. Everybody was fired up. It was a done deal. I was running for office. I thought, *Oh crap, I need to call Jane!*

It worked out well because Secretary Perry had always been a friend of mine, and I had a lot of respect for him. This turned out to be fateful as well. I knew I wanted to run, but I had never run for office and had no idea what I was doing. Perry immediately took me under his wing and put me on the path to win. He put me in touch with my new campaign consultant, Rob Johnson, who had run his gubernatorial and presidential campaigns. Brian also really helped me get the ball rolling. This was key because I was already months behind and had no time to waste.

I called the navy the day after I decided to run and told them I wanted to retire and run for office. I asked them what I needed to know. They said you can't run for office while you're on active duty. I knew this, but they also told me that I couldn't publicly talk about my plans to run or spend any money on a potential race until I was officially out of the navy. This meant I was dead in the water until I got out of the navy. The rule in the navy is you have to retire on the first day of the month. The filing deadline in Texas was December 9, which meant I had to be completely out of the military by December 1. That was six weeks away! It usually takes six months to get everything done and get out.

I was a little discouraged and thought, *Maybe I waited too late to do this? There's no way I can make this filing deadline, right?* I decided there was only one way to find out, *I have to get my stuff together as soon as possible and see if there's any way to make it happen.*

A couple of days later, I got all my retirement paperwork together and walked across West Executive Avenue to the West Wing. I saw the chairman of the joint chiefs and the secretary of defense coming out of the Situation Room. I walked up and said, "Mr. Secretary," and he said, "What's up, Doc?"

I said, "I'm going to retire, get out of the military, and run for office."

He said, "That's great!"

I said, "I have one problem, and I may need your help."

He said, "Sure, what do you need?"

I said, "I need to get out quick. I have to be out of the navy by the first of December."

They looked a little surprised. "That's just a few weeks away. That's a tight one, but get all your stuff together and push it through as fast as you can. Can't make any promises, but as soon as it hits our desk, we'll get it out of there and expedite it if we can." I got my package done and submitted Wednesday morning the following week, and by the close of business on Friday, I had retirement orders with a retirement date of December 1. Three days!

I retired from the US Navy after almost twenty-five years of active duty and simultaneously resigned from my role as White House chief medical advisor on December 1, 2019. Most people at the White House didn't even know I had left. One day I was there working, and the next day, I was gone. I didn't have time for a retirement party or any type of departure ceremony. I had a race to run, and I was way behind.

I spent the next week turning in equipment and getting read out of programs at the White House. On December 8, I flew to Dallas and picked up a new truck I had bought. I let Freddy Ford, President Bush's chief of staff, know that I was going to be passing through Dallas, and he suggested I stop by and see President Bush. I had told President Bush I was running back in October. He was excited for me and very supportive. He told me that I should talk to Karl Rove before I went any further and that Karl would give me some good advice. I knew Karl from the Bush days, and I knew he was all about Texas politics, so I thought that was a great idea. The next day, I got on the phone with Karl. To my surprise, he told me that there was no way I could win that race. He said the fact that I grew up in the neighboring district would be the kiss of death in that race. He told me not to waste my time. It was not the advice I had hoped for, but it did not sway me from moving forward. When I showed up in Dallas on the 8th, I went by President Bush's office as Freddy had suggested. I was glad to see him but was hoping he wouldn't ask me about my conversation with Karl. Of course, he asked me right away. He said, "What did Karl have to say?"

I said, "Well, sir, Karl wasn't very positive about it. He essentially said I didn't have a snowball's chance in hell."

He paused for a minute, then he said to me, "Ronny, the first time I ran, my dad had a guy just like Karl, and he said to me, 'George, you have to talk to this guy before you run. He is going to give you the keys to the kingdom.' You know what he told me, Ronny?"

I said, "No, sir, what did he tell you?"

He said, "He told me the same damn thing Karl told you. You know what I did?"

"No, sir, what did you do?" I said.

Then he said, "I ran anyway! Son, if it is in your heart, don't you let Karl Rove or anybody else talk you out of it."

It was outstanding advice. I had already decided I had to do it because I knew I would regret not giving it a try, and I would always wonder if I could have done it. But talking to President Bush made me feel much better about my decision.

The next morning, I got up, drove to Austin, and filed for office two hours before the filing deadline. I was officially in the race with fourteen other Republican candidates for the US congressional seat in the thirteenth district of Texas.

Needless to say, I was the last one in the race, and everyone else was months ahead of me with staffing, endorsements, fundraising, and everything else you could think of. I had reached out to a friend of mine, Jake LaGrone. Jake worked for Jason Aldean but had grown up in the Amarillo area and knew a lot of folks in the district. Jake and I got to know each other years before, during my time at the White House. I told Jake I needed him to connect me with someone in Amarillo who could introduce me to some of the key people involved in politics there. He reintroduced me to Chris and Kristi Morrow. I had met them at an Aldean concert a few years back. We had an absolute skeleton crew and no money. It was me, Jane, Chris, Kristi, and my consultant Rob. That was it! Chris and Kristi spent weeks driving me all over the Texas Panhandle, introducing me to hundreds of people. We started raising a little money. Jane was in her truck, driving all over the entire district, putting up signs, and meeting people. My new district was huge. It includes forty-one counties and is almost forty-two thousand square miles. It takes over six hours to drive from one side to the other if you don't stop! I was working sixteen hours a day, seven days a week. I was going to Walmarts, Home Depots, diners, churches, rodeos, and anywhere I could find someone willing to talk to me. I was winning over hearts and minds, one voter at a time.

I had a little bit of name recognition and celebrity based on my time as President Trump's physician, and that certainly helped in my new district. These were my people, and they were fans of President Trump just like I was. I only had the money for one ad on TV, so we made it count. The president hadn't officially endorsed me yet, but most people knew how he felt about me. This ad highlighted that with multiple clips of him saying positive things about me during some of his previous rallies. The ad spoke for itself. Then, on the last day of early voting, the president tweeted out, "Hey, let's get behind Ronny Jackson and get him into the runoff."

The top two candidates running against me sensed the momentum I had and started to get nervous. They had decided days before to gang up on me with negative ads, but it was too little, too late. Election Day was the following Tuesday, and I made it into the runoff.

It was early March, and now there were just two of us left to fight it out until the runoff election scheduled for May. COVID-19 was just starting to emerge, but it hadn't impacted the race up until that point. But after the primary, everything started to change. Businesses started closing, and it got increasingly difficult to go out and campaign at most public places.

I stayed as aggressive as I could and continued to go out as much as possible; even though many people were trying to stay home, I was still out. I still went around, and I knocked on doors. I continued to do campaign events. There weren't as many people showing up at the events, but I just kept trying to do more and more of them. My opponent was lulled into a false sense of security because he had beat me in the primary by almost twenty points, but it wasn't over, and I knew I could win. I could feel the enthusiasm when I spoke to people, and momentum was building exponentially. I just had to keep telling my story and making the case for why I should represent the district. My opponent pretty much stopped campaigning. That was a big mistake because if the runoff had been in May, as planned, there's a possibility that he would have won. I was still trying to get my name and message out, and I hadn't reached quite enough people yet. But due to COVID-19, the governor changed the runoff race from May to July, and this turned out to be the kiss of death for my opponent. He was a good guy, but unfortunately, I had all the momentum at that point, and now I had two more months to win voters over.

I started looking for a place to live in Amarillo in October 2019, as soon as I decided I was going to run. I requested that my terminal move in the navy be back to Texas, and, specifically, Amarillo. Immediately, my opponents tried to label me as a carpetbagger who hadn't lived in Texas in twenty-five years and didn't yet own a home in the district. I was born and raised in that specific part of Texas, and I maintained my Texas residency the entire time I was in the navy. Luckily the people in my district are very patriotic and appreciated the fact that the only reason I wasn't in Texas all those years was that I was serving my country all over the world, including in the combat zones of Iraq and Afghanistan. I knew this wasn't going to be a problem when one of my opponents tried to use it against me in a debate, and it totally backfired. He said, "You know I grew up here. My kids have gone to school in this school district their entire time in school. They'll graduate from here, and this is our home."

It was, of course, intended to point out that he had deeper roots in the district than I did, but it didn't come off that way in the end. I patiently waited until it was my turn to talk. Then I said, "That's wonderful; I'm glad that your kids have had the benefit of growing up in the same area all this time, with the same friends, and at the same school. Guess what? My kids moved nine times the first eleven years I was in the military. Every single year, my kids had to move to another school, make new friends, and have their whole life uprooted because I was serving my country in the military." I handily won those debates, and I never heard another word about it.

The night of the election in July, we had a really big watch party near my house in Amarillo. We were watching the early votes coming in, and it looked like I was winning almost all the counties with the early vote ballots. Things were looking good, but I didn't want to jinx myself; I was keeping my fingers crossed. By the time it was over, I had not only made up the twenty-point deficit I had from the primary, but I'd also added on another fifteen points for a thirty-five-point swing. We crushed it, and I won big! I started getting tons of calls from everyone at the White House. They had been tracking it closely and knew it was over before the press called it. Of course, President Trump called right away and spent quite a bit of time congratulating not only me but Jane and the rest of my family. All the hard work had finally paid off. It was a great night!

8.

Right from the beginning, I thought the partisan media hype over COVID-19 was being blown way out of proportion. I could tell early on that the Left was trying to take advantage of it for political reasons. They were spinning it and saw huge benefit immediately in the form of unsolicited mail-in ballots. I honestly don't think they thought they had any chance of winning the presidential election until COVID-19 came around. That was the first time many in the party thought, *Hey, we might be able to win this!* They wanted to tear President Trump down. They were looking for anything. They'd tried everything—Russia hoax, made-up mental and physical issues, and anything else they could get away with lying about. They thought, *Finally, this is going to be the big domestic disaster we can hang around his neck and destroy him with.* And if they couldn't find a way to blame him and impact his popularity, at least they had a great case for mass mail-in ballots all over the country and the follow-on ballot harvesting.

I don't know what advice the president was getting on the inside because I was out campaigning. However, I think President Trump did the right thing. He immediately put together an expert medical advisory group and listened to what they had to say. He shut down travel from China and Europe and restricted travel from our southern and northern borders. I would have said doing that makes sense until we figure out what's going on. Lock it down and determine the actual risk. Was this going to be the plague that everybody said it would be and wipe out half the Earth's population? No one knew at the beginning.

Initially, the president even followed their advice and encouraged the public to wear masks and social distance. The good news was, we quickly began to realize who the vulnerable populations were. The bad news was we should have made decisions based on that data, but instead, that is when the politics started to take over, and state and local Democrats let their newfound authority go to their heads. Asking people to social distance and wear a mask made sense early on before we knew if masks made a difference or who was at risk. It also made sense since we had no known treatment for the virus and no vaccine. However, once the vaccine was developed and several medications were found to be of benefit, the overall approach in the country should have shifted. And who do we have to thank for the vaccine? Donald J. Trump! His Warp Speed program was definitely out-of-the-box thinking that was a game-changer. Unfortunately, after he left office, the Biden administration completely mismanaged the vaccine program and made it political, like they do everything else. In keeping with their divisive identity politics, they tried to create two classes of Americans, the vaccinated and the unvaccinated, and pit them against each other. Shameful!

I am definitely not an "anti-vaxxer." I've taken vaccines my entire life, and I've had the COVID-19 vaccine. My kids have always had their routine childhood vaccines. But the use of any drug, vaccine, treatment, or procedure should be based on a risk-benefit profile for the individual, and that calculation and decision should be between the patient and their doctor. Not determined and mandated by politically motivated bureaucrats and politicians!

I fully understand this virus is very dangerous and potentially deadly for certain people. I've had a few of my close friends die from COVID-19. My parents are older and have comorbid medical conditions, and my sister is a transplant patient on immunosuppressive drugs. I told all three of them to get the vaccine the second it was available. We *should* be following the science. And the science says we should encourage vaccination, protect the vulnerable populations, and let the rest of the population live their lives and make their own decisions. The science says that the elderly, those who live in nursing homes and assisted living facilities, those with other significant medical illnesses, and the immunocompromised should get the vaccine. Their chances of dying or serious morbidity from the virus far outweigh any known or unknown risk of the vaccine. The science also says there is absolutely *no* reason to vaccinate our children. Children don't readily get infected or transmit the disease, and if they do get infected, they do not get seriously ill. This vaccine was developed using novel technology involving mRNA. I believe it is safe in the short term, but the reality is we *do not* know what the long-term effects of this vaccine are. This is especially important for developing children and women of child-bearing age.

I would have never advocated for keeping children out of school either. But once again, they wanted to scare everybody, and there was no better way to scare people than to have them think their kids might die from it. There was even a brief narrative created that we needed to worry about our pets getting COVID-19. What?

The fact that the Biden administration and Democrats all over this country have ignored the science and insisted on stoking the fears of everyday people and destroying the economy and the livelihoods of millions of Americans is unconscionable.

Trump was on the right path. He initially placed a lot of emphasis on his panel of medical experts, led by Dr. Fauci. But, as time went on and we learned more about the virus, vulnerable populations, potential therapies, and had a vaccine authorized by Emergency Use Authorization, he realized he had a national economy to protect as well, and there had to be a balance between public safety concerns and a sick economy. There *is* a such thing as *acceptable risk*. He established an economic advisory group to work with the medical group and provide the balance needed. Unfortunately, as soon as he left office, Biden immediately embraced the fear tactics and mandates that have done so much damage. And he even went so far as to put Dr. Fauci, who we now know had a pivotal role in developing this virus, in charge of it all.

The Biden administration has chosen to ignore the overwhelming number of people in the country with natural immunity. Millions of people have had the illness and don't need the vaccine. Some people got it and got pretty sick but recovered. Many people got it and only had cold and flu symptoms. An overwhelming number, including many children and young adults, got it and never even knew they had it. If it were really just about public health and not politics, documented natural immunity would count.

Why won't they acknowledge natural immunity? Because they want you to do what they say and not question their authority. I think this is all about control. It's not a liberal thing anymore; it's a Communist-Marxist thing. They need you to get accustomed to the government having complete control over your life. They need to ensure that fear exists and keep it stirred up as much as possible. Now, they're talking about the COVID-19 passport because they want you to get used to showing your papers. They want you to *prove* you're compliant before you are allowed to travel, go to a movie, go to a restaurant, or even go to the grocery store. They want you to have a government card that says you're vaccinated. It will ultimately give them total control over your life because that's just the first step. Pretty soon, you'll have to have papers for something else and then something else, and eventually, they'll own your life. It sounds crazy and extreme until you open your eyes and see what has happened to this country over the last year. Much of it would have been inconceivable to all Americans just a few years ago.

To this day, I don't trust the numbers out there. They'll tell you that many hundreds of thousands of people died from COVID-19. I don't believe it! Many of these people died from other illnesses but had an incidental finding of current or previous COVID-19 infection. That does not mean they died from COVID-19 or that COVID-19 even had anything to do with their demise. People were dying from heart attacks, strokes, cancer, even car accidents, and their deaths were being added to the COVID-19 death tally. The Democrats supported this during the Trump administration because it kept the fear level high and assisted in their efforts to blame Trump for the deaths. It was going to put them in the White House, which is what it ultimately did.

We even have proof of that now. We had a CNN producer saying that they put those numbers up because they were trying to tear Trump down and wanted those numbers to be as high as they could get them. Isn't it a little suspicious that as soon as Biden was sworn in, the banner CNN had on the television twenty-four hours a day with the *death toll ticker* was suddenly removed?

How did the government facilitate this? It was easy: they made it in everyone's financial best interest. I don't think there was any malicious intent initially, but it quickly became a useful tool that worked in the Democrats' favor. The goal was to help the hospitals and clinics that were dealing with the initial outbreak of COVID-19. The government created a financial incentive if COVID-19 was one of the diagnoses on the chart at hospital discharge or death. As long as the medical record was coded to reflect that the patient had tested positive sometime in the days or weeks before, during the hospital stay, or even had a presumptive diagnosis of COVID-19 without actual testing, the reimbursement rate went up, and they got paid more. The requirement was very liberal, and it also led to increased testing in asymptomatic patients. As such, it naturally inflated the numbers of COVID-19 cases and "COVID-19 deaths."

I'm in *no* way saying that doctors or hospitals were acting fraudulently, but the government definitely used a financial incentive to encourage COVID-19 testing and documentation by providers to increase reimbursement. This is nothing new. In the system we currently have, doctors and hospitals live or die based on their ability to survive in the world of government reimbursement.

There is also a big financial incentive for the private sector. Moderna is now telling us we need a third vaccine, a booster. They're going to make a fortune producing this vaccine for everybody on the planet! It's bullshit. There's not a single independent study out there that says we need a third vaccination. Where is the research? If the research is ultimately done by someone other than the company that makes the vaccine and it definitively demonstrates that immunity wanes after a certain period of time, then I will accept the notion of a booster. But currently, we don't have that. Unfortunately, those on the Left who say we should follow the science don't seem to need to see the evidence in this case. The Left is eating it up like, "Oh my God, yes, we should get another one."

I have a feeling that as soon as we get closer to the elections and the primaries, we'll suddenly start hearing about new strains that have come out and are super dangerous, that people ought to be terrified of, and we'll need to lock down again. If the Democrats are unsuccessful in their legislative efforts to federalize the election process and make unsolicited mail-in ballots the law of the land, they will need COVID-19's help again.

Now that I am in Congress, I split my time between Washington, DC, and my district in Texas. They couldn't be more different. In Amarillo, Wichita Falls, and everywhere in between, people are back to normal and going to events. Nobody's wearing a mask, and everybody's doing their own thing. And guess what, we are doing fine. I saw some moron running down the street in DC today: he was running all by himself at the edge of a park, and he had a mask on and a belt with hand sanitizer clipped to it. I couldn't help but think, *what an idiot*. The virtue signaling is comical. These people are sheep, and unfortunately, Biden has appointed Dr. Fauci as their shepherd.

Unfortunately, we'll never know exactly how or why COVID-19 arrived. There will never be an answer as long as Biden is in office because the Democrats will never investigate. They'll destroy anybody who tries to. I spent a large part of my time in the military dealing with, and preparing for, the threat of chemical and biological warfare. The fact that this virus came from a lab in China and was developed using gain of function methods is strong evidence that it was most likely part of a Chinese bioweapons program. I can't prove that, of course, but it certainly fits the image. It's common knowledge that the best way to weaponize a micro-organism is to create one that makes people very sick but does not kill them. If you do that, you not only take that person out of the fight but also all the people that have to take care of them. You also consume lots of money, equipment, and other resources in the process. Much more bang for the buck than simply killing someone. Sound like something you have seen? I am a firm believer that this was probably an accidental release from the lab in Wuhan, but I also believe it was probably part of an ongoing bioweapons effort. Unfortunately, it is looking like we, when I say we, I mean Dr. Fauci and NIH, may have unknowingly funded it. I don't think that Dr. Fauci and NIH knowingly funded a bioweapons program. But it is becoming pretty obvious that they funded gain of function research on *this* coronavirus in China. Evidently, we need better leaders at NIH and a lot more oversight!

Why won't Biden push China to investigate the origins of COVID-19? Probably the same reason he won't push China on anything since he has been in office. I don't know what that reason is, but it might have something to do with Hunter Biden. If you think the stuff you heard was on Hunter's laptop is bad, that probably pales in comparison to the dossier the Chinese and Russians have on him and his father. I think Biden knows this, and he'll do any damn thing they tell him to do. When I was at the White House traveling to places like China and Russia, it was common knowledge that there would be cameras in our rooms collecting information on us. Hunter traveled to these places extensively while his father was vice president of the United States; I am sure he was a prime target for these foreign intelligence collection agencies. I'm sure after all that time, they probably have stuff implicating Joe as well.

The sad part is China and Russia don't have to do anything to destroy this country except sit back and watch. Somebody said the other day that the biggest villain in American culture right now is America. That's what the Left has been teaching our kids for decades, and that's what they're teaching everyone now. It's sad but true.

The Far Left, the Democrats, and the mainstream media are fighting the war on behalf of our enemies. They are the flag bearers for the people who want to destroy us. They are watching us eat ourselves from the inside out, and they are doing everything they can to facilitate it. While we spend all our time engaged in battles that revolve around identity politics, racial hate-mongering, wasteful socialist spending, Marxist control of our lives, and countless other *America Last* policies, the Chinese are rapidly becoming both the economic and military superpower on the planet. Our current path suggests they will not take these dominant roles from us, but rather, we will give them away. Someday soon, the Left will have to answer for why they insist on helping those who want to do us harm. But in the meantime, I am going to do everything I can to stop them. We're not going to give up our country to the likes of AOC, Rashida Tlaib, and Ilhan Omar; we're not going to do that. That will never happen.

There can be *no* land of the free if we are not *the* home of the brave!

It's time for all America-loving patriots to stand up, fight back, and hold the line!

9.

FINAL THOUGHTS

In regard to the DoD IG report:

There's no nice or polite way to say this: It's a total bullshit political hit job.

It was January 21, 2021, just minutes after 12:00 p.m., which was precisely twenty-four hours after Joe Biden was sworn in as president of the United States. I got a phone call from the Department of Defense saying they had finalized the report and were forwarding me a copy. They informed me I had five days to reply. They also told me that once the five days had passed, the report would be released to the press. I was shocked. This investigation had been sitting around for over three years and was based on accusations that go back to eight years ago. I had been told before I retired that it was closed out. Apparently, they were resurrecting it. I did not have to ask myself, *Why now?* I knew. I was in Congress now, and Biden was in the White

House. It's the one tool in their toolbox they think they can use to try and destroy me, and now they believe they have top cover from the White House to do it. They currently have the House, the Senate, and the White House; they're going to take advantage of the situation and come after everyone they perceive as a Trump person, especially people like me.

I'm not only a Trump person, but after January 6th, I didn't disown Trump. I didn't walk away from him. I still supported the president and his Make America Great Again/Keep America Great agenda. I didn't back away like the Far Left, the woke press, and the "Never Trump" Republicans demanded. I became a primary target. They're coming after me now, recycling all the same accusations and garbage they put out when I was the nominee for the VA secretary.

My lawyer said we weren't replying to it. He said, "Ronny, you know this is absolute garbage. We're going to send them an email, tell them we have no reply, and send it to the navy. When the navy gets it and the navy decides what to do with it, we'll address it with the navy. We'll give them one more opportunity to do the right thing, and if they don't, we will go nuclear on them and put this to bed once and for all."

I also received a phone call stating the Department of Defense would be sending the report to the navy and releasing it to the Senate Armed Services Committee, the House Armed Services Committee, the Senate Veterans' Affairs Committee, and the House Oversight Committee, and it would also be posted publicly on their website. I thought, *The navy hasn't even seen it yet, and they're going to make it public?*

I specifically asked if it was normal procedure to release such a report to the public before it had been reviewed by me or the navy.

They told me it was not and that normally, it would go to the navy first and would not be released unless there was a FOIA request. At that point, it would be up to the secretary of the navy. They then proceeded to tell me that it had been determined that, due to my high-profile position in Congress, it would be released immediately. They would not tell me who made that decision.

If I had retired and not gotten into politics, this investigation would have never gone anywhere. They would have closed it out, and it would have been over and done with. I would have never heard another word about it. As a matter of fact, I was told just before I retired that it had already been closed out. This was happening because I am a perceived threat to the Biden administration and because a few political appointees in the Department of Defense want to make a name for themselves.

At the time of this phone call, there was an acting DoD inspector general, an acting secretary of defense, and an acting secretary of the navy. None of these people had been appointed yet, which means these people were auditioning for jobs. What better way to impress the Biden administration and be considered for a high-profile political appointment than to cut off the head of Dr. Jackson, a Trump guy, who was Trump's personal physician, and who is now a Republican congressman who is aggressively and vocally opposing Biden?

What better way than to take down one of Biden's most public enemies? Unfortunately, the Department of Defense, like other parts of the executive branch, is increasingly being used as a weapon against people with conservative views and those that don't share their new woke ideology. This creates an incentive, for many who work at all levels in the IG, to support the Far Left's political agenda for personal gain. That's really what this is all about. They want to destroy me, and they will probably give it their best shot, but they will not succeed. They are accustomed to people they go after not fighting back; they actually count on it. They know most people don't have the will or the resources to stand up to them. But I am not among that group! I was elected to this office, not appointed by the government, and the only people who can remove me are my constituents. And guess what, they're not going to. They see this for exactly what it is, complete bullshit.

Will it cost me some votes here and there? Probably. Will it gain me some new support here and there? Probably. Will it inspire some folks to donate time and money to my future race so that I can continue to serve in Congress and push back against Biden and the Far Left? Probably. I don't know; we'll have to wait to see how this all plays out. But the reality is, they're just trying to publicly tear me down because it's in their best interests on a political level.

The crazy part of all of this is the accusations are from way back in the middle of the Obama administration. Why did these people wait over four years before bringing any of this up? And why would President Obama have promoted me and appointed me as his personal physician well after these incidents supposedly took place? Easy, because they *did not* take place! In fact, President Obama handwrote my evaluations while I was on active duty in the White House, and his assessment of me, my character, my professionalism, my performance, and my leadership could have not been more glowing and positive. Not only that, but when the accusations first came out, while I was in the Trump administration and the VA nominee, many senior members of the Obama administration immediately came to my defense. Most privately, but many came out publicly.

Denis McDonough, who was President Obama's chief of staff and is now President Biden's secretary of the VA, called me after all the accusations came out and told me to hang in there and that my friends from the Obama years had my back. Denis also made calls for me during the nomination process in support of my nomination. Alyssa Mastromonaco, President Obama's deputy chief of staff, and David Axelrod, senior advisor to the president, both came out publicly with tweets and posts on social media, saying, "This is ridiculous; we've known Ronny Jackson for a long time; there's no way this is true." There were others as well. They were good friends, and I appreciated their courage in defending me. To be honest, now that I am one of the most conservative members of Congress, they don't all care for me so much now. But I guess that is just the way it goes when you have to get in the fight the way I have. I still consider them friends.

The one person who could have made the biggest difference by simply picking up the phone and making a single call to Senator Jon Tester but hated Trump so much he couldn't do it? Barack Obama!

Obviously, I was never a fan of the Obama administration's policies, but I did get along with everyone on a personal level and enjoyed their company, President Obama included. Once I started working for President Trump, I began to lose friends from that time in my life pretty quickly, including President Obama.

The first time I ever criticized Joe Biden online, I got a somewhat scathing one-page email from President Obama, telling me how disappointed he was in me.

Jane and I were driving from Amarillo to Wichita Falls to attend a campaign fundraiser, and Biden was on TV again, making crazy statements and concerning mental gaffes; he didn't know what state he was in or what office he was campaigning for. He apparently thought at one point that he was running for the Senate and later couldn't remember what state he was campaigning in. This had been going on for months and was getting worse. I was listening to some of this on the radio and reading about it on social media while Jane was driving. I was getting a little frustrated with the ongoing double standard and how Biden was treated compared to President Trump. Nothing new, we are all accustomed to the mainstream media bias regarding the Democrats, and the love fest with Biden as the nominee had been underway for a while now. I was taking this one a little personally since the press and the Far Left hacks had previously involved me in their false narrative and lies about Trump's mental capacity. Trump never made crazy statements like the ones Biden was making almost every day, but these people were jumping up and down: "He's not fit to be president; he needs a cognitive test!" They were demanding that from now on every president be required to submit to an exam by a panel of psychiatrists to prove that they're mentally fit to be president. I told Jane, "I can't believe all those people in the press and the so-called doctors in academia who came after me and Trump are not saying something about all this. This is ridiculous! Where are those people now?" Right about that time, I saw somewhere on social media a tweet in reference to Biden's latest cognitive misadventure with an attached video.

When I saw that, I thought, *This is unbelievable! I've got to say something about this.* So I retweeted it with a message that said something like: *Remember the cognitive test that I gave @realDonaldTrump? The one he aced! Sounds like somebody else might need some testing done!!*

Scary!! And that was all I said. Well, within twenty minutes of me sending that, I got a scathing email from President Obama:

> *Dear Ronny,*
>
> *We haven't spoken in a while. I hope you and your family are well.*
>
> *I have made a point of not commenting on your service in my successor's administration and have always spoken highly of you both in public and in private. You always served me and my family well, and I have considered you not only a fine doctor and service member but also a friend.*
>
> *That's why I have to express my disappointment at the cheap shot you took at Joe Biden via Twitter. It was unprofessional and beneath the office that you once held. It was also disrespectful to me and the many friends you had in our administration.*
>
> *You were the personal physician to the President of the United States as well as an admiral in the U.S. Navy. I expect better, and I hope upon reflection that you will expect more of yourself in the future.*
>
> *Barack Obama*

Needless to say, that email surprised me.

I was already late to the fundraising event, and everybody was waiting on me, so I thought, *Okay, I'm going to this event first, and then I'm just going to think about what I'm going to say, and I'll email him back*. Then I thought, *I'm not going to email him; I'm going to call him, and I'm going to talk to him.*

I'll admit, I was a little flustered by the email and very distracted during the fundraiser. I hadn't heard from him in a long time, and the email caught me off guard. I knew he must have been pretty pissed because I got the email just a few minutes after I sent the tweet. I finished the event, and I was just about to pick up the phone and call him when I decided I would run it past a couple of good friends who had worked with me at the White House while I was with President Obama. There are only a few people who would really understand how I was feeling. It was somewhat of a mixture of hurt feelings and pissed off. The first person I called was Dan Bongino. Dan had been a good friend of mine for many years, and I knew he would know how I felt, and I knew I could trust his judgment. He quickly set me straight. He said, "You do not owe him a phone call. You were getting butchered in your nomination with the VA, and did he pick the phone up? One phone call from him to Tester or anybody on the committee, and it would have been dead in the water. You would have gotten confirmed as secretary of the VA or at least they would have backed down, and they wouldn't have tried to destroy you with those allegations. He had the opportunity to help you, and he didn't lift a damn finger. Screw that guy!"

So, upon reflection, I thought, *You know what? Screw that guy! I'm not doing it.* I just walked away from it, which was the last time I had any contact with him.

* * *

Imagine that. A kid from a little West Texas town named Levelland, with a population of slightly over ten thousand, was being rebuked by a former president for criticizing the future president because he didn't like that I worked for the current president. All the while, I was headed to my first fundraiser as the next congressman from Texas. But just as the trajectory of my own life has taken unexpected twists and turns, so, too, have the challenges facing our nation evolved and grown more complex. As the controversy over the pandemic continues, as the socialist government takeover threatens our basic freedoms, and as the political division seems to deepen by the day, it is imperative that we have leaders who stand up for what they genuinely believe to be right. I served this country in Iraq. I continued to serve it under three presidents. And I serve it still to this very day. I've held more titles than I could have ever envisioned back when I was just trying to stay out of trouble in my youth—doctor, assistant to the president, navy admiral, physician to the president, and now congressman. But I am an American first and foremost. And I will continue to hold the line for my constituents—now more than ever.

ACKNOWLEDGMENTS

To my wife, Jane, and my three children, Libby, Ben, and Matt. I would be nothing without you all in my life.

Jane, you have always been there for me no matter what the situation. You are the rock in my life that has always kept me anchored and headed in the right direction. In doing so, you have always carried your load and often mine as well. You stayed home, worried about me, and made sure our family had everything we needed while I deployed to desperate and dangerous places like Iraq and Afghanistan. You stayed home and dealt with all the mundane day-to-day tasks while I stayed in five-star hotels and flew all over the world on Air Force One, and you never complained a single time. You always made my career one of your top priorities, and I would not have a career or a family without you. THANK YOU!

Libby, Ben, and Matt, no matter where my path leads me, from this point forward, I feel I have succeeded in life because of you. It is a great thing to be envious of your own children's success. Thank you for always having my back, and I hope you are lucky enough someday to have children just like the three of you. I could not be prouder to call all three of you mine. Oh, and now I have a fourth that I am extremely proud of as well—my new daughter-in-law, Arden.

To my father, Waymon, and my mother, Norma. Thank you for always being there for me and for always working overtime to keep me on track. You are great parents who knew when to be hard on me, but never left any doubt regarding your love and support. You gave me all the tools for success and provided the example of how to make it all work. I owe you everything.

To my brother, Gary, and my sister, Stacy. I could not have asked for more supportive siblings. You are both great friends and were great partners growing up. You have always been there when I needed you. When I made the decision to run for office and become one of the more outspoken and polarizing conservative members of Congress, you were both unexpectedly thrown into the fire by association. Thank you for always defending me and bearing the burden with me. It is nice to have a brother and sister that never let you feel alone.

I want to thank the many friends, shipmates, and coworkers I had during my twenty-five years of active duty in the Navy. In particular, those I served with during three presidential administrations and almost fourteen years in the White House. Thank you to Captain Jeffrey Kuhlman for pushing my early career along and setting me up for success. We did not always see eye to eye, but I wouldn't be here without his early trust in me. Deep appreciation to my most trusted mentor, Brigadier General Richard Tubb. Dr. Tubb hired me as the junior physician during the George W. Bush administration and later in my career became one of my best friends and biggest supporters. To Keith Bass, my deputy in the White House, and later the director of the White House Medical Unit. Keith, I would have crashed and burned a hundred times without you. Thank you.

Thank you to the three presidents I served. I learned much from each, and they were all wonderful to work for. Thanks most importantly to President Donald J. Trump—my president! He trusted me to be more than a great military physician and to lead at the next level. He believed in me enough to nominate me as one of his key cabinet secretaries and ultimately encouraged me to run for Congress and make a difference on a bigger scale. Thank you, Mr. President!

With regards to this book, thanks to Johnny Russo and Erik McKenna for spending hours putting my words to paper. Having never authored a book, I could not have gotten started without you both. Thank you to Anthony Ziccardi, my publisher, and to Maddie Sturgeon, my editor, for your patience and for making it all happen. And last, but definitely not least, thank you to my longtime friend Dan Bongino for introducing me to all the fine folks at Post Hill Press.

8/22